KW-052-042

HOW TO RE-ENGINEER YOUR PERFORMANCE MANAGEMENT PROCESS

HOW TO RE-ENGINEER YOUR PERFORMANCE MANAGEMENT PROCESS

FRANKLIN HARTLE

First published in 1995

Kogan Page Limited
120 Pentonville Road
London N1 9JN

British Library Cataloguing in Publication Data

A CIP record for this book is available from the British Library.

ISBN 0 7494 1640 8

Typeset by Saxon Graphics Ltd, Derby
Printed in England by Clays Ltd, St Ives plc

Contents

Preface

It is not an easy task to write a book about performance management which claims to add something new. The publishing world is littered with hundreds of books on the topic. But we believe that there is something new to say on this subject and more importantly we are convinced that it is worthwhile saying. We believe in the value of an effective performance management process. Equally, we realise that there is much work to do to ensure that all performance management arrangements really do deliver what they promise.

Part 1 deals with the current state of play with the use of performance management in organisations in the United States and Western Europe. It defines performance management, assesses how well it is doing, how organisations are changing and discusses the implications of these organisational changes on traditional approaches to performance management.

Part 2 outlines the steps you can take to re-engineer the traditional approach into a more effective performance management process.

The book draws from real case studies of work with Hay clients in the United States, the United Kingdom and other Western European countries. It is written primarily for the users of performance management, ie all line managers and employees. It is this audience that can make performance management really work. We believe that for performance management to be fully effective it has to be a collaborative exercise between managers and staff. It is not, or should not be, a process which is 'done to you'. We should all accept the responsibility of 'making it work'.

Acknowledgements

This book could not have been written without the help of my colleagues in the Hay Group. My thanks to them for the use of their materials drawn from their performance management work with clients in many different countries. My particular thanks for their encouragement and support to Murray Dalziel, Helen Murlis, Tjerk Hoogmiestra, Debbie Dean and Deborah Coombs.

Part I

Assessing the Current Situation

Chapter 1

What is Performance Management?

A DEFINITION

Before you move on to the rest of this chapter think about what 'performance management' means to you. Take a few minutes to write down everything which you associate with the words:

Performance Management

Probably you have written down a long list of words, such as:

Appraisals	Time consuming
Objective setting	Bureaucratic
Merit pay	Paper driven
Plans	Top down
Progress reviews	Peer appraisal
Annual cycle	Getting clarity
Ratings	Feedback
Development	Recognition
Team working	Upward appraisal

This experiment was tried with a group of middle managers in a UK manufacturing company during a performance management workshop and they produced the list of words above. The comprehensive nature of the list illustrates that there are many different words which we associate with the concept of performance management. It is a widely used, and sometimes abused, term. Some organisations use it in a narrow sense to refer to 'performance appraisal' or 'performance related pay'. In these organisations the performance management arrangements are focused around the appraisal meeting and the financial pay-out; these are the main 'drivers' for the process and the reasons for its existence. In other organisations there is a broader definition – such as 'the way we manage our business'. Here it is regarded as an on-going management process. To a large degree performance management is what you want to make of it. However, you might find that the following definition is helpful:

> **a process for establishing a shared understanding about what is to be achieved, and how it is to be achieved, and an approach to managing people which increase the probability of achieving job-related success.**

Why might this definition be helpful? Let's highlight a few of the key words used in the definition:

Performance management:

- ***is a process.*** Not just a set of forms which are routinely completed or the annual appraisal ritual, or the bonus scheme. It is about the everyday actions and behaviours which individuals take to manage performance improvement in themselves and others. It cannot be divorced from the management processes which pervade the organisation generally.
- ***is for establishing a shared understanding about what is to be achieved, and how it is to be achieved.*** To improve performance individuals need to have a common shared understanding about what performance (and success) in their job looks like. Whether it is a set of tasks, objectives or results; or a set of behaviours; or a combination of both. They need to be defined clearly and by

agreement with the job holder so that people know what they are working towards.

- ***is an approach to managing people.*** The focus of performance management is on people; it is about how individuals and teams work together and support each other to achieve shared aims. In particular, it puts the responsibility on managers to work effectively (through coaching and motivating) with those for whom they are accountable.
- ***increases the probability of achieving job-related success.*** Performance management has a clear purpose – it is about achieving success in the work place for individuals and the organisation in which they work. It is about achieving wins for everyone.

By establishing a continuous management process which delivers clarity, support, feedback and recognition to all staff, you will take a major step in ensuring significant performance improvement of your organisation.

THE REASONS FOR UNDERTAKING PERFORMANCE MANAGEMENT

First let's examine some aims set out by other organisations.

A City Council

The performance management scheme has been introduced for two reasons:

1. to improve the performance of the authority, with particular focus on the clear identification of priorities and objectives, and their successful achievement;
2. to help individuals to enjoy their work and develop their potential to the full.

A Retail Store

The appraisal process should result in:

- the setting of individual objectives that conform to businesses' and individual needs;
- the improvement or maintenance of an individual's contribution within the full limits of the job, and their effective development;
- the improvement of an individual's performance by identifying and putting right obstacles that restrict that performance, as well as building on 'strengths';
- the implementation of agreed action plans that will lead to improvements in performance.

A Healthcare Company

'The management of people will be a key priority for the future and will be facilitated through the performance management process. It will enable us to manage the performance and the potential of our people in a planned and constructive way, and will play a key role in releasing and developing everyone's full capability.'

A City Technology College

'Performance Management is part of the strategic management process which will link people and jobs at every level of the College organisation to the stated mission and objectives of the College ....'

A National Vocational Education Organisation

- to ensure that the performance of employees is geared towards the fulfilment of the organisation's objectives;
- so that all employees know what is expected of them;
- to encourage personal development in this context.

A County Council

- ❑ People are more motivated to achieve objectives which they themselves have helped to establish.
- ❑ People are more likely to achieve results which they believe are important.
- ❑ People work more effectively where they know, and have helped to plan, what they are expected to achieve.
- ❑ They can improve their performance when they understand the processes of monitoring progress and measuring results.

A Major Utilities Company

'The prime reason for introducing performance management is to provide a greater concentration on corporate performance. It will do this by linking the company's strategy and plans to individual jobs.

This means greater direction from the top in specifying key corporate and business unit targets. It means greater personal accountability on the part of all senior managers for translating these into work-unit targets and ensuring that they are achieved.'

A County Council

'We exist to provide quality services to the people in our county. As a service organisation we are crucially dependent on the quality, skill, motivation and performance of all members of staff. To help achieve this we have developed performance management and pay processes which seek to ensure that all staff are aware of the part they play, and that their individual contribution is fully recognised.

Appraisal forms a key part of the overall process of performance management and is your right. It represents a partnership to ensure that your full capabilities are realised to achieve high quality services.'

These definitions illustrate that many organisations are beginning to see the performance management process as a dynamic 'real time' feature of organisational life. In these organisations (such as the County Council above) performance management is regarded as an integral and essential part of the day-to-day delivery of the organisation's business and not as a separate stand-alone process.

Defining what *you* want from performance management

What you hope to achieve through the performance management process should have a significant impact on what kind of process you design, and the people who will participate in it.

Take a few minutes to think about what your organisation wants from performance management. Look at the lists below which set out the potential benefits that can be derived from performance management and match your objectives to them.

Business Objectives	*Tick ✓*
❑ increase focus on key business objectives	
❑ alignment of organisation, department, and individual objectives	
❑ reduce costs	
❑ raise productivity	
❑ support a total quality management initiative	
❑ support an 'Investors in People' initiative	
❑ improve or maintain particular standards	
❑ implement a new project or structure eg team working	
❑ achieve other specific business objectives	

Human Resource Management Objectives	
❑ improve communication about business objectives	
❑ increase employee commitment to the organisation	
❑ improve managerial capabilities	
❑ change to a more focused 'performance culture'	
❑ improve retention of staff	
❑ increase staff motivation	
❑ change dominant managerial styles within the organisation, eg empowering	
❑ introduce performance related pay	
❑ increase focus of training through clearer definition of training needs	

❑ increase managers' focus on their 'management' roles
❑ provide better ways of assessing individuals' performance to fit people to roles and managing careers
❑ achieve other human resource objectives

Individuals' Objectives

❑ more clarity about what performance is expected
❑ more regular feedback on how they are performing
❑ understand clearly how managers view their performance
❑ define more specific training to meet their needs
❑ have an opportunity to discuss how the manager has managed them
❑ define more specific development to meet their needs
❑ identify career development opportunities
❑ get better rewarded for their contributions
❑ increase opportunity for more to participation in decision making
❑ achieve other objectives

Probably you have ticked off quite a few items. Most organisations seem to have a long list of desired outcomes for the performance management process. In a UK survey of nearly 2000 organisations in 1992 the Institute of Personnel Management[1] found that the most common reasons were as shown in Table 1.1.

The most common reasons focus on the fact that the performance of the organisation rests on the achievements of the individuals who work within it.

Table 1.1 *Reasons for Introducing Formal Performance Management Programmes*

Reason	% of organisations with formal schemes
Improve effectiveness of organisation	85
Motivate employees	57
Improve training and development	54
Change culture	54
Link pay to productivity	50
Attract and retain specialists	45
Support TQM	36
Link pay to skills development	16
Manage wage bill	14

The theory of performance improvement through performance management goes like this:

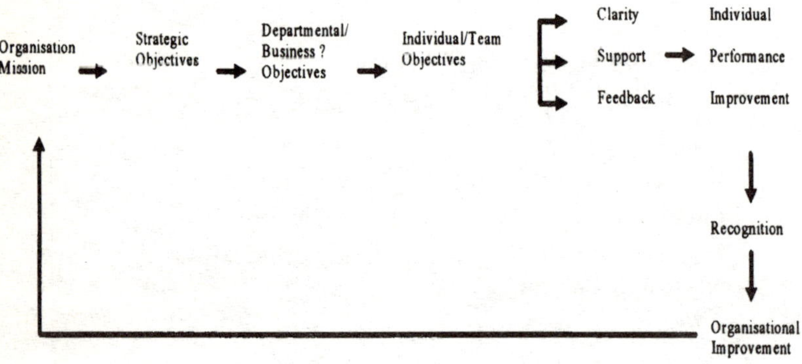

Performance management has much potential to change organisations. Effective performance management can increase motivation, management capability, open up communications, change attitudes and behaviours and create a more performance-oriented culture.

But it cannot achieve everything. You should not be over-ambitious for the process. There is a danger of setting a too-demanding agenda for a single process. It would be more effective to focus upon the three or four key areas you really want to change or improve through the development of a performance management process.

Striking the Right Balance

In drawing up a list of priorities you should aim to strike a balance between meeting the needs of the organisation and the needs of employees. They are not mutually exclusive.

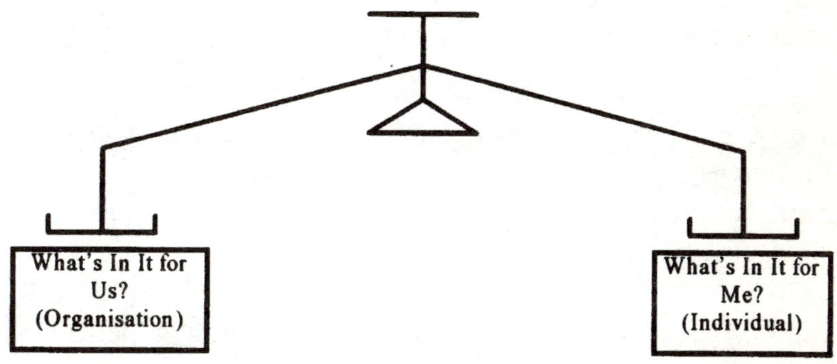

Better Planning (Alignment, Focus) — Clarity about what to do

Better Communications (Horizontal, Vertical) — Better dialogue with manager and colleagues

Improving Managerial Capabilities (Objective setting, Motivation, Communications, Coaching, Feedback) — Better quality management, feedback and support

Empowering the workforce — More freedom to decide on the 'What' and 'How' of performance

Focused development planning — Structured framework for developing performance and potential

Better value for money (on payroll costs) — Better recognition for doing good work

Improved performance at all levels — An opportunity to meet expected performance in a structured and consistent way

The most effective performance management process is able to meet some organisational objectives and some individual needs.

DEFINING WHAT SUCCESS LOOKS LIKE

Having identified your priorities then you should define what success should look like for each priority, ie how will you know when you are achieving each priority? For example, if you have identified as a priority – 'improving the business planning process' – then you might define success by such factors as:

- ❑ business objectives set by end of November;
- ❑ all staff aware of business objectives through regular team briefings;
- ❑ all individual objectives aligned to corporate businesses' objectives.

The list of priorities and the definitions of success give a set of success factors for the entire performance management process.

Reference

1. Institute of Personnel Management (1992): *Performance Management – An analysis of the Issues* IPM, London

Chapter 2

Diagnosing Your Performance Management Process

NATIONAL SURVEYS IN THE UK

In the United Kingdom in 1992 the Institute of Personnel Management[1] conducted a survey of nearly 2000 employers to establish the effectiveness of current practice in performance management. Altogether 46 per cent of the organisations returned questionnaires covering a total of 4.3 million employees (just under 20 per cent of the UK workforce). The main conclusions of the survey were:

1. Just under 20 per cent of the organisations claimed to operate a formal performance management system. A further two-thirds (66 per cent) of employers were operating other policies (not called performance management) to manage employee performance and 14 per cent had no policies to manage employee performance. The most common arrangements were referred to as 'performance appraisal', the focus of the process being on the once a year formal appraisal of performance.

2. Employers with formal performance management schemes were more likely to be implementing other processes as well, eg total quality management (TQM) and performance-related pay (PRP).
3. Altogether nearly three-quarters of the organisations in the survey had some form of performance-related pay. However, there was no correlation between use of PRP and whether an organisation was considered to be 'high-performing'.
4. Performance-related pay was considered to be most effective when sitting alongside a performance management process. However, several case studies suggested that overall organisational performance could be improved without PRP being part of a performance management process.

This is a very important conclusion – ie performance management *on its own* can improve organisational performance; performance can be worsened by performance-related pay where it is introduced without an existing performance management process.

This survey highlighted that the main focus in the development of performance management in most UK organisations has been on performance-related pay, and that, without performance management to support it, it was not being effective in the majority of organisations.

However, in another UK survey in 1990, the Local Government Management Board undertook research to discover the benefits and drawbacks of performance management in local authorities. In its report[2] it concluded that many local authorities considered that performance management was raising performance levels, managers said that it had 'sharpened up performance', encouraged 'greater dynamism' and that 'it forced you to do good things'. *What stood out was a conviction that performance-related pay alone was not raising performance because a cash incentive was not motivating people to work harder, but that a performance management process had communicated priorities and reinforced the kind of behaviour the organisation wanted.*

So the main conclusions to be drawn from these national surveys of performance management/performance-related pay arrangements in the United Kingdom are that:

1. Performance management arrangements were found in many organisations, but there were significant differences in how they were designed and how effective they were.
2. Most performance management schemes were centred upon the appraisal process and were driven by the links to pay.
3. Among the personnel managers there was generally a positive view of performance management. In those organisations where it was working effectively the benefits were listed as:
   - greater clarity of what they should be achieving and how to improve their performance;
   - better support and coaching from their managers;
   - systematic and constructive feedback on how they were doing;
   - more focused training and development;
   - more recognition (formal and informal) for what they have achieved.
4. Many managers and employees were not so confident that performance appraisals and performance-related pay arrangements alone improved performance. Indeed, there was evidence that without proper design and careful implementation they were almost certain to hinder individual and organisational performance.
5. In those organisations where the performance management arrangements were only partially effective, the most commonly quoted reasons were:
   - 'managers do not take it seriously';
   - 'it takes up too much time';
   - 'it is too bureaucratic';
   - 'it is not related to the real issues of the organisation';
   - 'it is only bits of paper';
   - 'we were never properly trained';
   - 'ratings are inconsistent and unfair';
   - 'objectives are unreal and unrealistic'.

In the worst cases the 'performance appraisal' was regarded only as an administrative burden. In the words of one senior line manager in a UK clearing bank: 'Performance appraisal is a load of rubbish. You decide on the rating you want in the box, and then make up a few words of the narrative to justify it.'

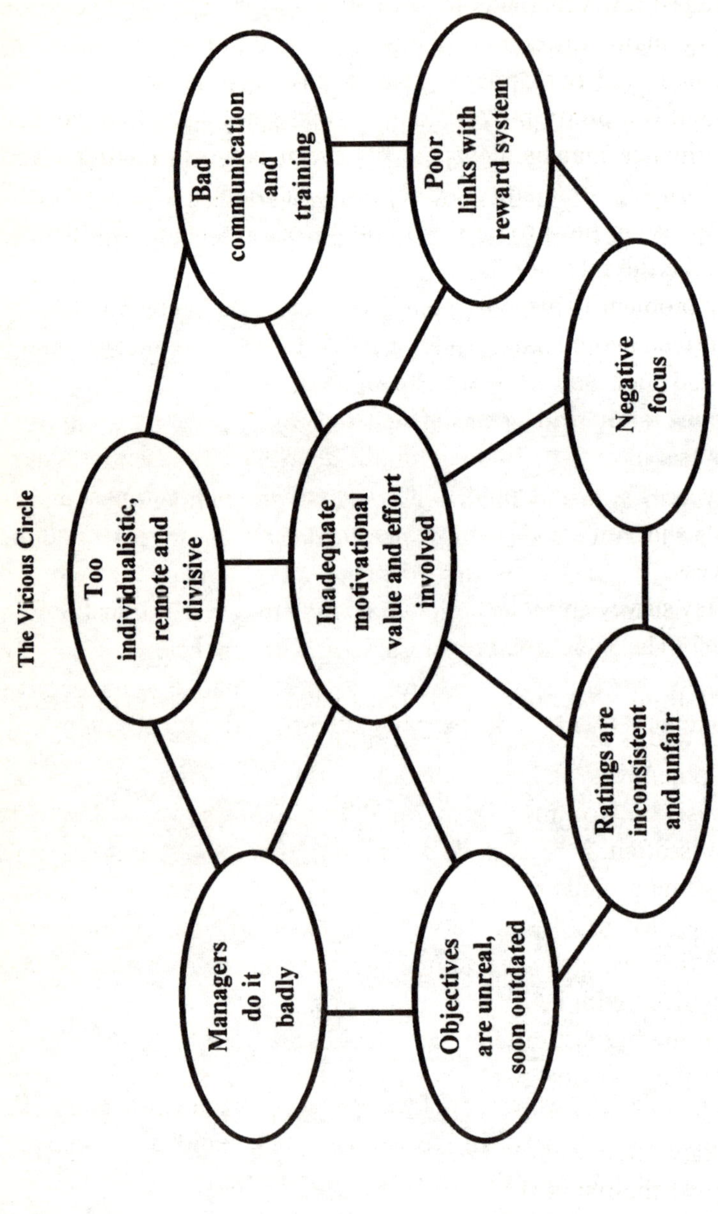

Figure 2.1 *What do employees feel about performance appraisal?*

Hay surveys

Over the last few years Hay has run attitude surveys and discussion groups in many different organisations about how performance management and performance-related pay are working. What we have found is a pretty mixed picture. Most employees like the idea of performance management and believe it is worth having – and also performance-related pay. But they are unhappy with what actually happens on the ground. 'Fine in theory but poor in practice' seems to be the message.

A key problem is that too often the process has become much too system-driven and bureaucratic. Invariably there is a manual – full of every good idea you have ever thought of – but not exactly user-friendly and rarely read by all staff. Then there is a series of documents or forms that have to be filled in (duplicate/triplicate) at set times during the year. The whole process has become too paper-driven, and is regarded as just an annual event rather than an integrated and continuous process.

The Hay surveys revealed other problems too. These are captured in Figure 2.1 (The Vicious Circle).

- ❑ People think that appraisal is too focused on individual performance and is divisive. It is frequently remote from what they do; their objectives against somebody else's objectives, not much emphasis on working together and building effective teamwork.
- ❑ There is often a 'black hole' at the top of the organisation – top management tends to regard performance management as something needed for people below ('they wouldn't be top managers unless they were successful managers'!) and consequently do not get involved with it.
- ❑ One of the biggest problems is the fact that managers often do it badly; they do not give recognition for good performance and they do not deal with poor performance constructively. Worse still, they often seem too busy to give time to manage the performance of their staff throughout the year.
- ❑ Poor communication of what performance management is for and how to get the most out of it.

- ❑ A lot of employees feel that agreed objectives are unreal, they do not have much relevance by the end of the year and nobody bothers to update them during the year.
- ❑ A lot of employees believe that ratings are inconsistent, unfair, sometimes biased against women or minorities and they are forced into patterns of distribution that may not fairly reflect the performance of the organisation or the individuals within it.
- ❑ Some employees feel that appraisals have a negative focus; they are about search, find and punish rather than the far more positive reinforcement of success; ie backward- rather than forward-looking.
- ❑ Many employees think that there are poor links with the reward system – they do not see a real, credible link between what they are asked to achieve and what they get paid in either pay increases or bonuses.

Survey after survey shows that performance management and performance-related pay have been under-performing. Not because they are regarded as poor processes, but because of the way they have been implemented. There is an all too familiar list of negative outcomes that goes like this:

- ❑ people are not clear enough about what good performance looked like in the first place;
- ❑ people are not clear what the 'extra' reward is for;
- ❑ the 'extra' reward is not motivating – being for many people an extra 1–3 per cent of base salary;
- ❑ managers do not always welcome the idea and so set unsatisfactory objectives, fail to track progress and provide coaching when required, do appraisals of hugely variable quality and do not really discriminate between employees on pay decisions;
- ❑ rating drift is proving a continuing problem and over-focus on rating for pay purposes is detracting from the developmental side of performance management;
- ❑ the motivational value from performance-related pay is pretty limited, even if the value in terms of personal recognition is sometimes been better than anticipated.

But despite these criticisms, there is no general retreat from the introduction of these processes, particularly in the United Kingdom. In those organisations which have worked at it year after year, and especially those who have put real efforts into performance management and who now, perhaps, say – 'well it is just the way we do things around here' – there is evidence of general performance improvement. You cannot of course prove it was performance management and/or performance-related pay that delivered this. Pay has often felt like a very crude lever – but it has somehow needed to be there. The challenge over the next few years is to get the right balance between performance management and performance-related pay. The pay link should be the supporting process; it should not be the driver for the performance management process.

Conclusions

1. From these surveys it is tempting to be pessimistic about the performance of 'performance management' in many organisations. Few management processes seem to be so universal and yet so maligned. Yet there is a paradox. Many employees like the idea of effective performance management – they appreciate the potential benefits it can bring; but the reality for most of them is different. Something has gone wrong in the implementation of the process in many organisations so that generally it is not delivering what it promises to deliver.
2. Many employees have been on the receiving end of narrowly conceived and poorly delivered 'appraisal' schemes which have failed to motivate and have not resulted in improved performance. Most users agree that the yearly ritual of criticism, praise – and then raise – hasn't done much to increase performance levels.
3. Many organisations have underestimated the level of managerial skills needed to provide support to the effective management of performance. In implementing the process many managers have been ill-prepared in terms of the development of technical skills and a thorough understanding of the process. Their 'hearts and minds' have not been won over.

Where are you now?	Score			
Attitudes	1	2	3	4
1. We have clear reasons for having Performance Management				
2. Our senior managers are strongly committed to PM				
3. Line Managers understand and work well with PM				
4. This organisation has a clear sense of direction and purpose				
5. People in this organisation are in no doubt that performance is what matters				
6. We have a clear idea of what support PM requires and who should provide it				
Skills				
1. Individuals are clear about what is expected of them in their jobs				
2. My manager and I agree what my priorities are				
3. We are used to setting goals for ourselves				
4. Managers motivate staff to develop and achieve their goals				
5. Timely and effective feedback/support is given and received				
6. We have a development programme to improve management skills				
Processes				
1. The business planning process provides a clear focus for our activities				
2. Business needs and priorities are well-communicated through the organisation				
3. Monitoring standards of performance is a regular management activity				
4. The current appraisal process has clear links to the business planning process				
5. The current appraisal process helps to improve performance				
6. Performance rating standards are fair and consistent				
Total score				

Score index
1 = Strongly disagree
4 = Strongly agree

Figure 2.2 *A mini-diagnostic questionnaire*

4. But there are positive indicators too. Performance management is working well in some organisations. A well designed and well implemented performance management process does help an organisation to define better its priorities and allocate people and resources accordingly. It can improve performance, motivation and the delivery of services.
5. To be fully effective performance management needs to focus on employees' short- and long-term development needs and it must give employees an indication of how performance can be improved.
6. Performance management can be introduced and operated with or without performance-related pay.

DIAGNOSING YOUR CURRENT ARRANGEMENTS

The challenge for those organisations whose performance management arrangements are not working fully effectively is how to re-engineer them so that they deliver greater value.

The first step is to diagnose your current situation so that you will have a clear and detailed picture of what is working well, what isn't working well and what needs to be revitalised. This section describes how you can carry out an audit of your current arrangements.

Three methods of diagnosing your current performance management arrangements are set out:

1. A mini-diagnosis.
2. Diagnosing the review phase of performance management.
3. Diagnosing the whole process.

A mini-diagnosis

For a quick and effective snapshot of how well your current arrangements work, try the mini-diagnostic questionnaire in Figure 2.2 which is set out on the page opposite. Decide on who to consult and ask each employee to complete the questionnaire.

Add up the scores for attitudes, skills and processes and produce a total score (it should not exceed 72!). If you score below 36, there are many issues which need to be tackled and you should look closely at the scores for individual items to guide you where to take action. A score of 36–54 suggests some issues to be addressed. If you score above 54 you have a solid foundation for the performance management arrangements and only need to take action if any individual items score 1 or 2 only.

This is a very effective tool to use with employees from different departments in the organisation or with individual managers and their teams. It is not a full diagnostic tool and should not be used when you need an in-depth audit of your performance management arrangements.

In a recent exercise with a group of middle managers in a production company the following scores were recorded:

Department	Attitudes	Skills	Processes	Total
Personnel	18	18	17	53
	17	19	18	54
	20	21	19	60
Engineering	12	17	16	45
	13	18	15	46
	12	16	16	44
Finance	18	16	18	52
	12	14	12	36
	16	12	14	42
Production	12	12	12	36
	10	10	14	34
	12	10	12	34

What conclusions can be drawn from these results?

1. Marked differences between departments (Personnel being far higher scores than any other department – not surprisingly since they had been driving the process in the organisation and had taken extensive steps to prepare managers and staff for the process).

2. Some departments, eg Production, revealing a consistent set of low scores (36 and below), suggesting major issues around the effectiveness of performance management arrangements in that department. This needed further investigation.
3. One department – Finance – having a mixed set of scores (52 ➧ 36) which suggests that a particular unit within the department might be having a largely negative experience of performance management. This needed further investigation.

In order to determine which actions might be necessary to improve the effectiveness of current arrangements, it is worthwhile to examine the complete scores for each item, eg:

	1	2	3	4
1. Clear reasons for wanting PM	✓✓✓✓✓	✓✓✓	✓✓	✓
2. Our senior managers are strongly committed to PM	✓✓✓✓✓	✓✓✓✓✓	✓	✓
3. Line managers understand and work well with PM	✓✓✓	✓✓✓✓✓ ✓	✓✓✓	
4. This organisation has a clear sense of direction and purpose	✓✓✓	✓✓✓✓	✓✓✓✓	✓
5. etc.				

(✓) = number of responses

The grouping of the scores for items 1–4 suggests that these areas need attention before you can develop more favourable attitudes to performance management.

Auditing a key phase of the performance management process

In this example a public sector organisation evaluated how employees felt about the annual performance review meeting.

The group of reviewees were asked to think about their last performance review and on a scale 0 to 10, to rate the review (0 = a very poor experience; 10 = a brilliant, well-run, helpful experience).

Part 1: Assessing the Current Situation

	Please tick as appropriate	Strongly disagree	Disagree	Not sure	Agree	Strongly agree
1.	I was given sufficient advance warning that I was to be interviewed last time					
2.	From my point of view I undertook sufficient preparation					
3.	The interview took place at the agreed time					
4.	My manager seemed to have prepared sufficiently					
5.	The atmosphere during the interview was generally friendly and helpful					
6.	I did not feel threatened in any way during the interview					
7.	I was given the chance to say everything I wanted to during the interview					
8.	My manager listened to what I had to say					
9.	My manager was frank with me during the interview					
10.	My performance was not criticised by my manager during the interview					
11.	My personality was not criticised during the interview					
12.	Proposals for action on my part were discussed during the interview					
13.	The proposals for action were agreed between us					
14.	I felt I wanted to improve my job as a result of the interview					
15.	My job performance has improved since the interview					
16.	I feel happier in the job since the interview					
17.	My relationship with my manager on a day-to-day basis is good					

Figure 2.3 *Diagnostic of the performance review meeting*

The distribution of scores was:

0	1	2	3	4	5	6	7	8	9	10
-	-	1	1	3	2	2	1	-	-	-

In our experience most organisations average 5–7 which is a reasonable score, but it could be better. A useful follow-up to this exercise is to ask those who scored the 2s and 3s why they scored it so low (typical responses are likely to be 'inadequate notice; poor preparation by manager; short meeting (10/15 minutes)'; 'the manager told me to read the form and sign it – there was no real exchange of views'; 'indifferent attitude by the managers'). Quite a horror story! Also you could ask high scoring reviewees to explain why their mark is high – they would probably list good practice points such as: adequate notice; good preparation by both parties; informal and constructive atmosphere; agreed agenda; two-way dialogue; consensus on performance achieved and what to do next year; a positive, professional meeting.

A more comprehensive picture of the effectiveness of the review meeting can be obtained by using the questionnaire set out in Figure 2.3. This is designed for reviewees, and basically presents a checklist of 'good practice' for performance reviews. It is a very effective way of monitoring performance reviews and of being able to locate where poor practice is taking place.

Recently this checklist was completed by 80 reviewees in a public sector organisation in the United Kingdom and these were the results:

Over 50 per cent of the respondents agreed that:

- ❑ they were given sufficient advance warning of the staff review meeting;
- ❑ they undertook sufficient preparation for the review;
- ❑ the interview took place at the agreed time;
- ❑ the atmosphere was generally friendly and helpful;
- ❑ they did not feel threatened in any way during the review;
- ❑ they were given the chance to say everything they wanted during the review;
- ❑ their manager listened to what they had to say;

- ❑ their manager was frank with them during the review;
- ❑ their performance was not criticised;
- ❑ proposals for action were discussed during the review;
- ❑ their relationship with their manager on a day-to-day basis is good.

Over 50 per cent of the respondents did not agree that:

- ❑ their manager seemed to have prepared sufficiently;
- ❑ proposals for action were agreed between them and their manager;
- ❑ they wanted to improve their job as a result of the review;
- ❑ their job performance has improved since the review;
- ❑ they have felt happier in the job since the review.

These results were encouraging. Most of the reviewees were saying that the reviewers have got most things right (notice; preparation; tone; dialogue; day-to-day relationships) and yet the actual review did little to inspire them to do things differently or better. One reviewee commented 'my manager goes through the motions, but his heart doesn't seem to be in it. He is doing it because he has to, not because he wants to'.

Turning around this situation is not just about developing the review skills of the reviewer. It requires action to change the reviewers' attitudes to the review meeting (and probably to raise their awareness about the basic principles of effective performance management).

As a result of the survey (and discussions with managers) a set of actions were put in place:

- ❑ revised guidance notes (on effective review practice) were re-issued to all staff;
- ❑ workshops covering objective setting, coaching and 'how to motivate staff' were provided for all reviewing managers.

Examples of diagnostic questionnaires for the planning/managing phases are found in Appendix 1.

A diagnostic of the whole process

If you have been operating a performance management process for some time it could be timely to diagnose the whole process. A diagnostic questionnaire is included in Appendix 2. A full diagnostic should invite views from managers and their employees and should be supplemented with focus group discussions with a sample of managers and staff.

Exercise

Below is the analysis of performance management questionnaires completed by over 200 managers in a large insurance company in the UK. The company was dissatisfied with the working of its 5-year-old performance management process across the organisation. Look at the response data for each question and draw your conclusions for each statement.

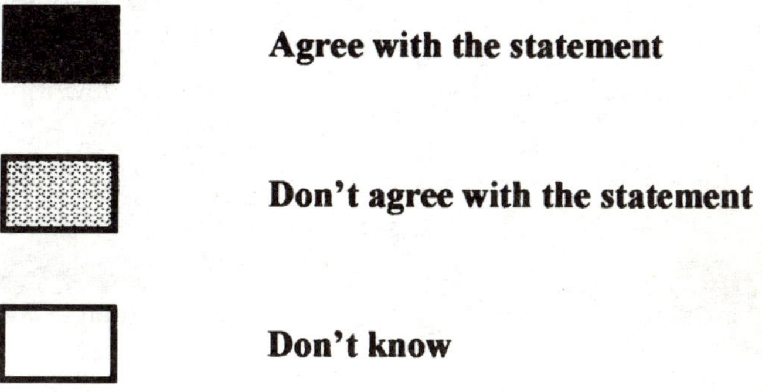

Links with pay

Pay - General

I expect an annual pay increase at least as much as inflation.

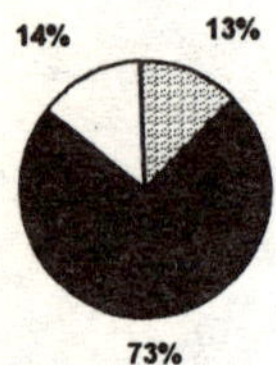

My manager is able to use the current pay system to motivate me.

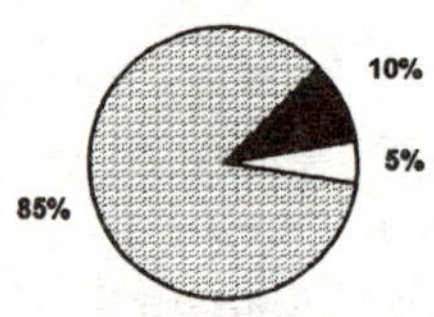

Pay could be used more effectively to motivate me.

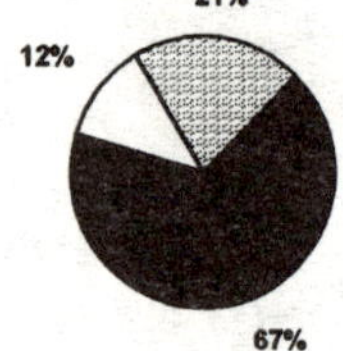

Pay Levels

My overall pay and benefits increase at least as much as inflation.

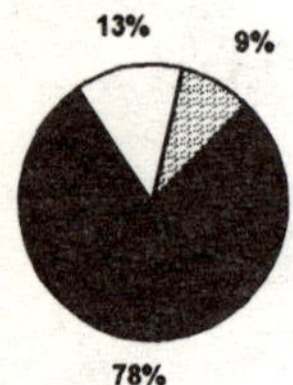

Pay could be used more effectively to motivate me.

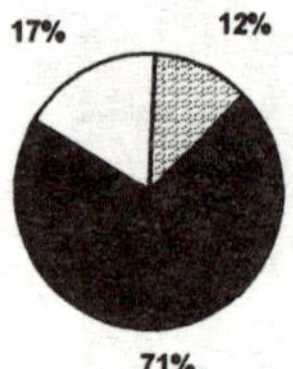

Performance Related Pay

It is clear how my annual performance appraisal links to my pay.

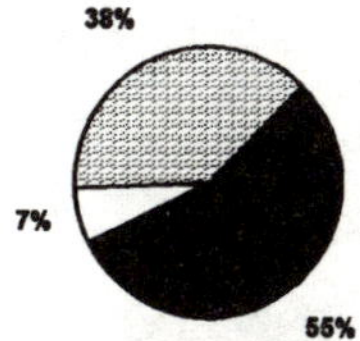

I feel my pay is a good reflection of my performance.

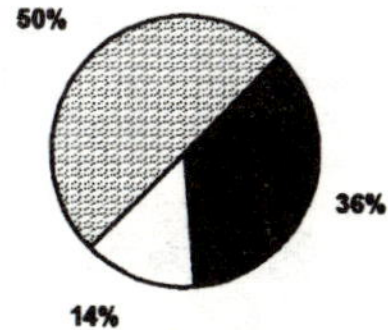

If I had performed poorly I would not expect a pay increase.

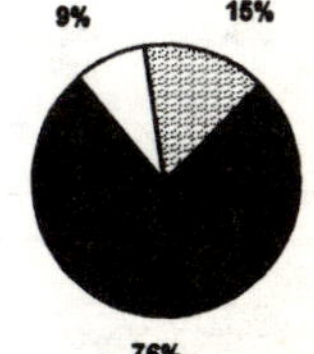

Pay Levels

Employees who are better performers should receive meaningfully higher pay awards than average performers.

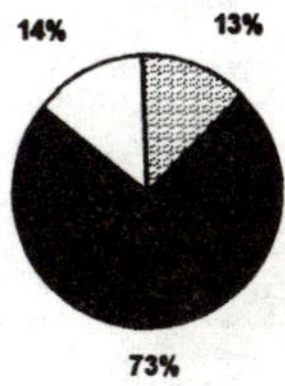

The current performance related pay system has been clearly explained to me.

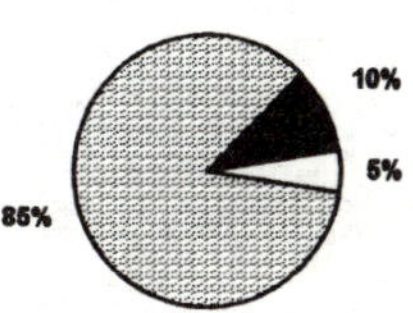

The current performance related pay system encourages better individual performance.

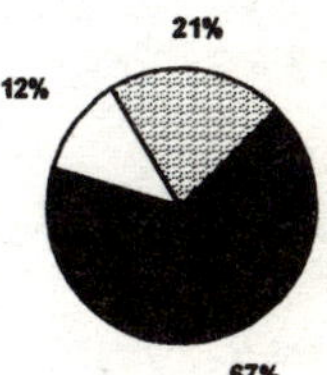

Organisational Arrangements

Structure and Design Making

The lines of responsibility and authority in this organisation are clear.

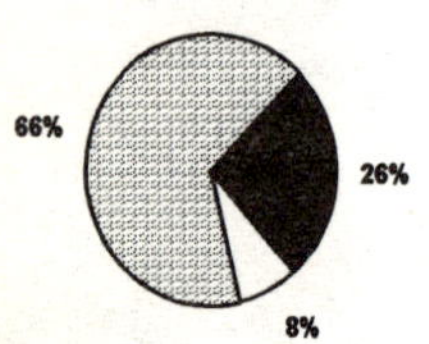

I can influence decisions which affect me.

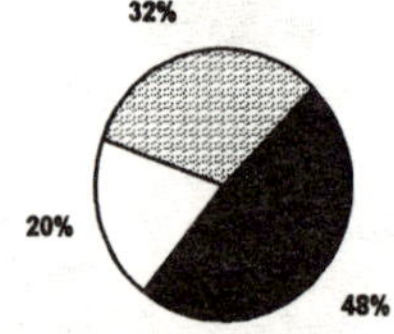

I can take appropriate decisions within the context of my job without seeking approval.

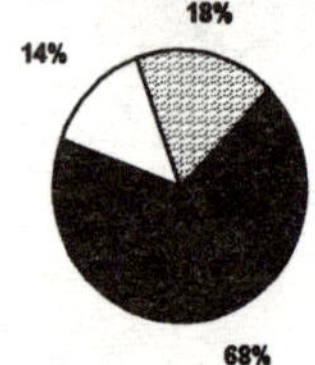

Technology and Teamwork

The computer technology I have access to substantially increases my effectiveness on the job.

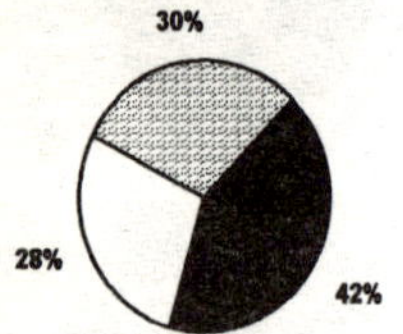

Effective teamwork is essential if performance is to be maximised.

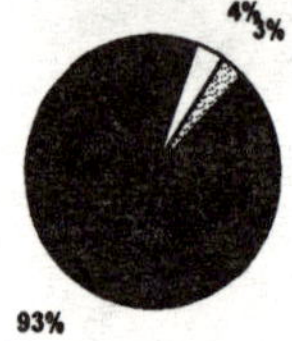

3. Performance Management - Effectiveness

People receive regular feedback on how they are performing.

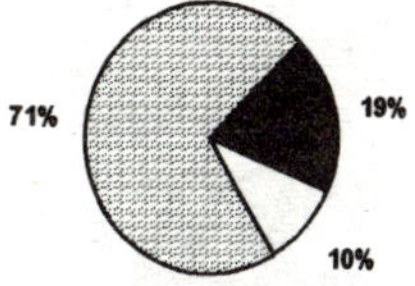

Poor performance is clearly visible.

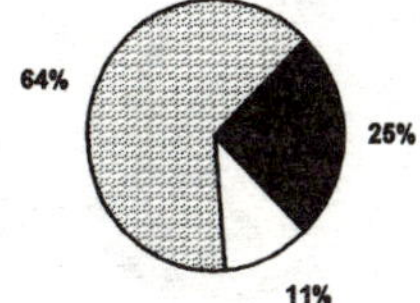

Poor performance is truly not tolerated.

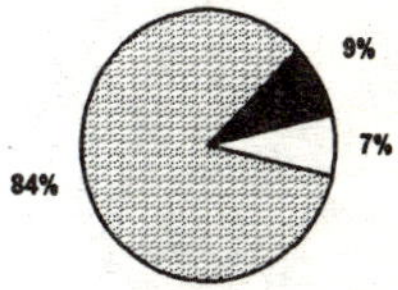

The best performers are clearly identifiable.

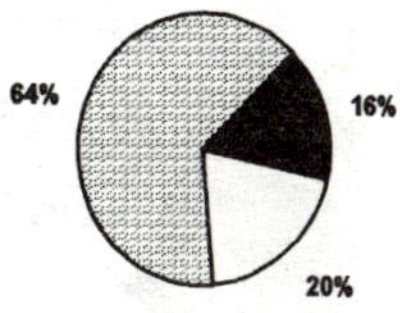

My performance review for salary adjustment purposes reflects my actual performance.

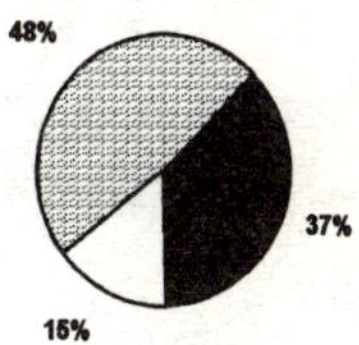

4. Performance Management - Understanding

I understand how my role contributes to the organisation's success.

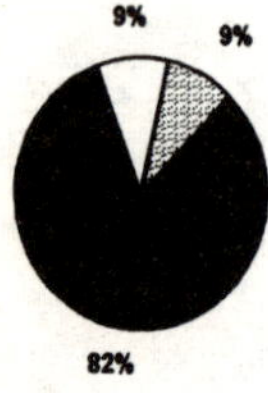

I know what the organisation's goals are.

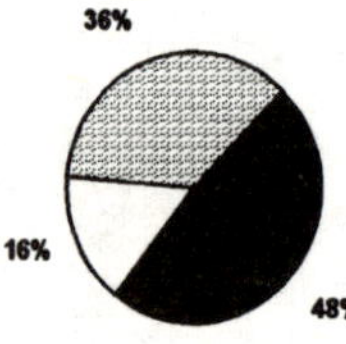

I understand how my actions impact on the organisation's performance.

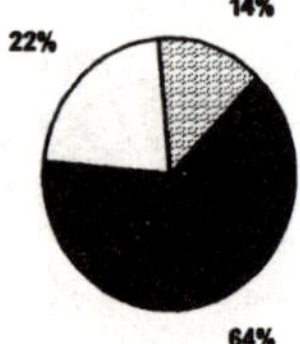

The best performers are clearly identifiable.

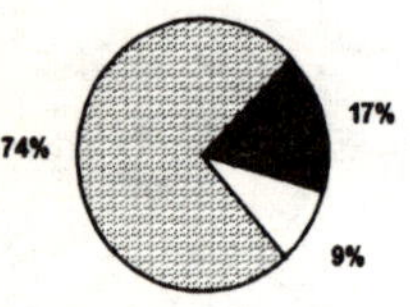

My performance review for salary adjustment purposes reflects my actual performance.

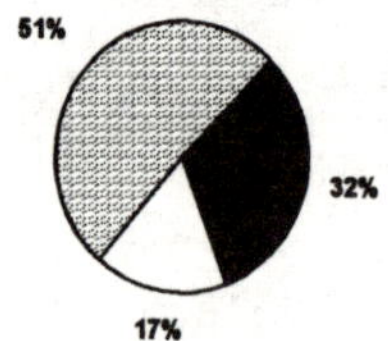

5. The Culture of the Organisation - Performance Orientation

This organisation places a high value on achieving profits.

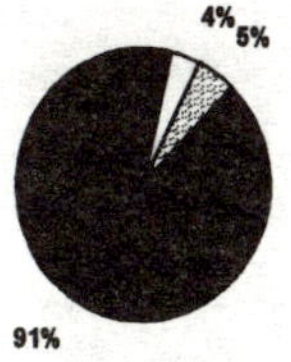

People are in no doubt that performance is what matters.

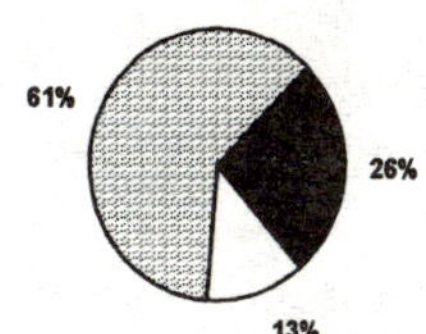

There is strong pressure to meet budget targets.

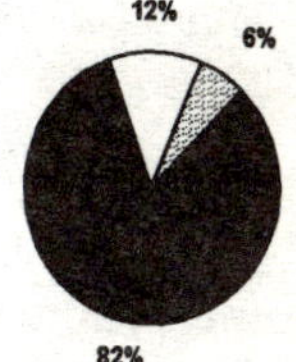

6. Performance Management - Clarity

I am clear about the end results expected in my job.

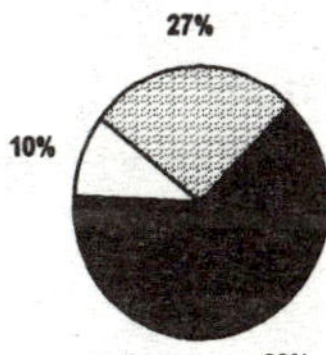

There are clear measures which could be used to monitor my individual performance.

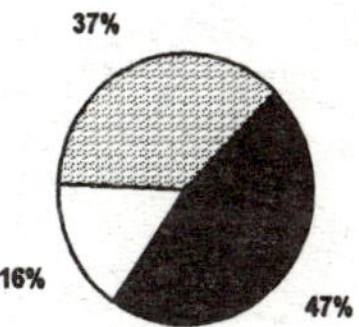

I am clear how my performance is judged.

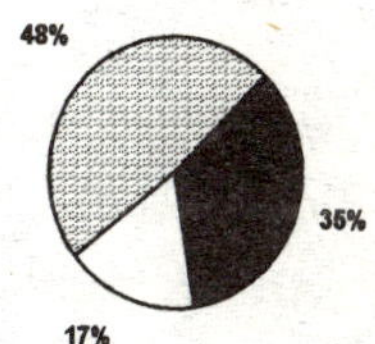

These are the conclusions of the consultant:

1. Very clearly oriented towards making profits and meeting budget targets but not a picture of 'performance' beyond these indicators. Not a real 'performance culture' yet; probably individuals could get away with not achieving targets.
2. People are clear about the end results expected in their job and many (about half) understand the measures which could be used to monitor performance. But general uncertainty about how performance is judged.
3. Seems to be a good understanding about how roles fit into the organisation's success and goals. There is a need for better communication of the organisation's goals.
4. Some problems with current appraisals (ie how performance is reviewed). Performance is not differentiated (could be problem with ratings definitions and/or unwillingness of managers to differentiate between employees; need to check ratings distributions across organisation). Clearly the appraisal meetings are not helping the majority of respondents to improve performance.
5. People are not receiving regular feedback on how they are performing. Poor performance is tolerated by managers and colleagues, although it is not clear how poor performance is identified.
6. Some issues about organisational clarity – lines of responsibility and authority are not clear to the majority. Most people say they have appropriate freedom to act.
7. Managers not using the current pay system to motivate. A large majority of staff feel that it could be used more effectively.
8. The majority seem to be clear how annual performance appraisal links to pay but feel that the reward does not seem a good reflection of individual performance. Wide acceptance that poor performers should not be given a pay increase.

So what actions need to be taken to address the shortcomings of the current appraisal system? Here are some actions which were recommended by the consultant:

❑ Make a stronger link with the business planning process. The performance management process should be the vehicle to clarify, communicate and deliver business objectives. Individuals should set their objectives following briefings by line managers on the organisation's and department's objectives.

❑ Managers should receive training in three areas:
  1. How to help employees define expectations in job (eg setting objectives).
  2. How to give coaching and feedback.
  3. How to carry out effective performance appraisals.

  A total of four days for each manager spread over the first year of new process.

❑ All employees to receive further guidance on setting job expectations. Job profiles to be prepared for a variety of jobs, including secretarial/clerical.

❑ Re-design the performance-related pay links. Make it more impactful and motivating:
  - mixture of organisation/team/individual rewards.
  - develop measures of performance for 'team working'.
  - allow managers more discretion to give one-off payments throughout the year (to reinforce good performance as it happens).
  - redefine the ratings definitions. Discuss with appraising managers how to apply the definitions.
  - address inconsistency in ratings distributions across different departments. Set up internal task force to monitor ratings.
    1. Prepare employee handbook setting out new approach to performance management and performance related pay.
    2. Prepare 'roadshows' for all employees to explain new process. Ask senior managers to make the presentations.

❑ the new process to be known as performance management not performance appraisal.

References

1. Institute of Personnel Management (1992): *Performance Management – An Analysis of the Issues* IPM, London
2. Local Government Management Board (1990) *PRP in Practice – A Survey of Local Government* LGMB, London

Chapter 3

The Changing Shape of Organisations

THE PRESSURES FOR CHANGE

We are in a period of significant change for all organisations. During the last twenty years mounting competition in domestic and international markets and fundamental structural change in much of the public sector has driven employers to look for greater flexibility and productivity and a stronger focus on serving the customer. There is no reason to believe these changes will go into reverse: if anything they will intensify.

These pressures are experienced by organisations in all sectors of the economy. Restrictions on public expenditure growth in the UK have led to radical structural changes in the public sector. Privatisation, Next Step agencies, Trust Hospitals, and opted-out schools have their roots in the competitive pressures in a more open economy. They have transformed their business operations.

Decentralisation, delayering and *rightsizing* are words that pepper the management language of the 1990s and are likely to do so well into the 21st century. And as structures change so too must the management behaviours which make the structures work. These new behaviours must reflect the organisation's wish to be more responsive to customer needs and to be more flexibly organised.

During the 1980s many organisations became more 'performance-oriented'. There was an increased focus on defining the outputs of jobs, and on linking job performance to the objectives of the organisation. This was the era of 'management by objectives'. Performance management began to grow out of its 'appraisal' box; there was an element of planning for performance. The way in which people were paid was changed too – so that there was an element of performance-related pay – usually in the form of 'performance bonuses'. Unfortunately many organisations have not moved on – they are still operating this old performance management process even though other aspects of their structure and management processes might have changed significantly.

So where are organisations going? What is the organisational pattern for the future? It is clear that flexibility of work and providing good quality services at lower costs, are becoming the key factors as organisations struggle. Successful organisations will be those who maintain 'continuous improvement' as a core value. Survey after survey of chief executives, senior line managers as well as human resource directors, all say that true competitive advantage will come from getting greater discretionary effort from employees – employees are seen as the most important asset. For companies to survive and prosper in the 1990s, new ways of motivating employees, and of managing the work climate of organisations, are critical. Successful organisations will be characterised by 'empowered' rather than 'command and control' environments and will provide a climate which encourages innovation, flexibility, team-working and quality of delivery. They will be customer rather than supplier driven. They will adopt team working and networking approaches and rely increasingly on the specialist knowledge of their workers and the ability of their managers to 'add value' by harnessing and developing that knowledge. Increasingly managers will have to build and manage teams that cross functional boundaries and which may last only as long as the immediate task. Because of delayering, they will have to deal with more information and take on more responsibilities.

The characteristics of these empowered team-based organisations will be those shown in Figure 3.1.

Work is defined through outputs at team level and individual capability drives job design.
Work is valued through broad bands of levels of contribution; competence and output based criteria. Individual development is encouraged.
Performance management through individual performance agreements; ongoing change/flexibility and key behaviours. It is the key management process to deliver business vision.
People are rewarded through smooth performance-related base pay progression and individual/team performance bonuses.
Individual and collegiate relationships become the cultural norm; management is visible but not intrusive.

Figure 3.1 *Empowered, team-based organisations*

In these kinds of organisations the human resource policies will need to be fully linked to the strategic drives of the organisation, reinforcing management styles, key behaviours and the work climates. Performance improvements will be achieved through continuous coaching and self-development – a true 'learning organisation'.

Not all organisations will want to go down the 'empowered, team-based' route. Each organisation must work out what 'shape' best fits its business and the environment on which it is working. The shape chosen should fit your particular work culture and this in turn should influence how you organise your supporting human resources systems. Hay/McBer have defined four types of work cultures (see Figure 3.2). These are:

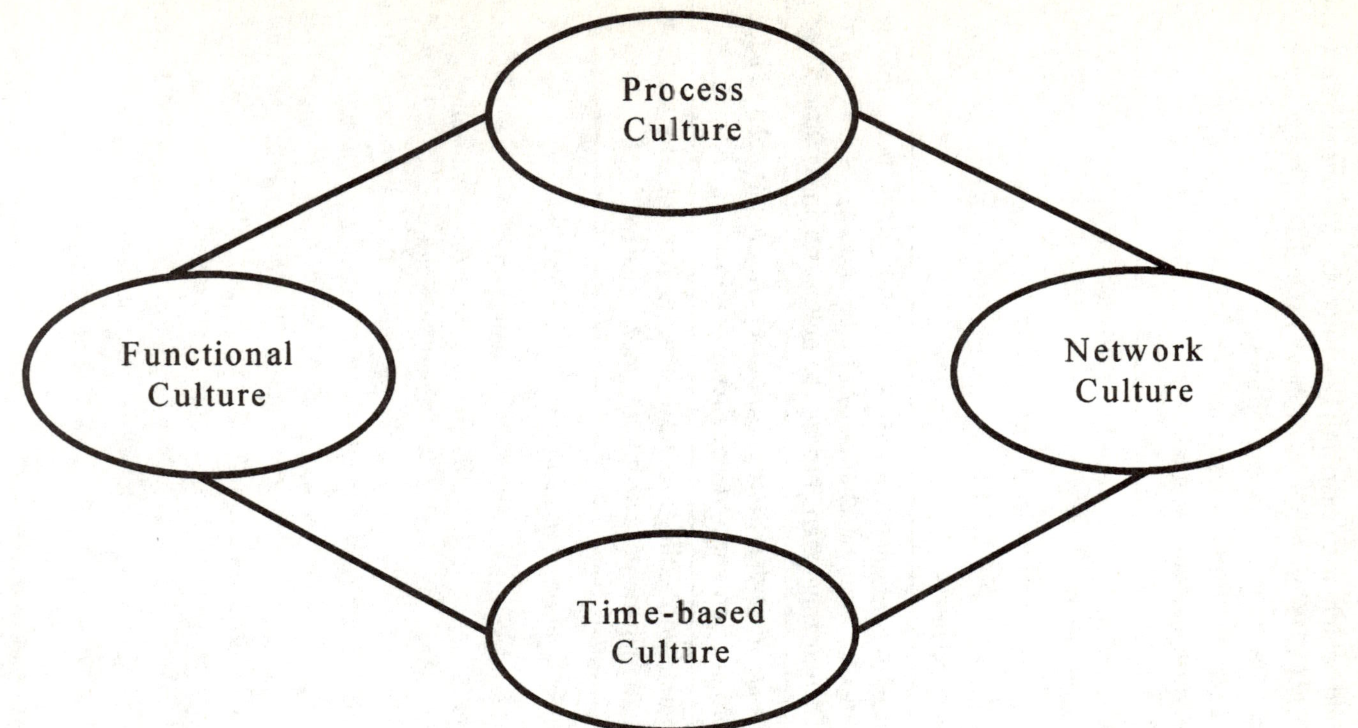

Figure 3.2 *Work culture models*

1. **The functionally excellent organisation** which gets its competitive advantage from finding and applying specialised knowledge;
2. **The process organisation** which gets its competitive advantage by organising its total stream of business around delivery to the customer or markets;
3. **The time-based organisation** which gets its competitive advantage from its speed of delivery to the market and ability to satisfy speedily changing customer preferences;
4. **The network organisation** which is organised around highly autonomous work groups which have not necessarily a stable relationship with each other over time. These organisations exist to adapt to constant change.

In each of these work cultures the shape and emphasis of the human resources systems including performance management will be different. (This issue is developed in Chapter 9: Fit with Work Cultures.) The important lesson for the future is knowing where you are going, what shape you want to be and what competencies/ behaviours will be critical for your success. Then you can design the organisational arrangements and supporting processes which will help you to reach your goals.

For most of Europe, the labour supply will not expand significantly in the next twenty years. The number of older workers will increase rapidly, particularly towards the end of the period. Educational standards are advancing in both developed and developing countries with some countries, including France and Korea, publicising their aims to educate at least 80 per cent of young people to 'A' level equivalent standard. Germany has already exceeded this target. In Britain the target is that by the end of the millennium over 50 per cent of all 18 year olds will be continuing into higher education. However, by the year 2000 over 80 per cent of the UK workforce will have already left full time education and up to a half of those already in work could still have very poor qualifications or no qualifications at all. The key point is that the increased competitiveness of UK organisations will not be decided by well qualified young people coming into the workforce, but by those already in employment.

Against this background it is even more critical that the talents and motivation of the existing workforce are developed and harnessed. They will require more training and personal development. They will need opportunities to 'grow' in their jobs, and to enjoy good 'teamwork' relations. Organisations will need to reinforce such qualities as initiative, team working, customer service and flexibility, by sound human resource management policies.

The picture which emerges when we put together these various features is one of 'leaner and fitter' organisations in both private and public sectors, with more flexible structures and processes, made up of more diverse and autonomous units, with a greater focus on team working and tailored work climates.

It is against this general background that performance management should be seen as a core management process – capable of delivering the business vision by developing and reinforcing the key behaviours/values. There will have to be an increased awareness from all managers of the skills required to manage and lead people so as to get the best from them ('the discretionary effort'). They will need to adopt a more influencing, facilitating and coordinating role and to develop new leadership competencies. They will need to manage in ways which improve the effectiveness of their staff by the development of motivating work climates.

Organisations that can do this will be the ones that derive competitive advantage, and will be successful organisations. This is the real challenge of the 1990s; these will be the organisations that will get a real return from investment in their key resource – developing the competencies of their people.

Chapter 4

The End of Performance Appraisal As We Know It

Given the evidence of widespread dissatisfaction with traditional forms of performance appraisal and the direction in which many organisations are changing, it is not surprising that many organisations are not just tinkering with their performance appraisal systems. They are transforming them.

In an industrial gas manufacturer in the United States, performance appraisal problems came to a head in 1989. Like other organisations involved in quality initiatives, the company found that its appraisal process was totally out of harmony with its new quality focus. While the company was trying to create a culture to empower employees and encourage teamwork, the existing performance appraisal process reflected a past culture of control and hierarchy. This is how the HR director described it: 'A one-way discussion from manager to subordinate. From the employee's perspective, it was a fairly passive event, based on objectives set 12 months before. Theoretically it linked up with our compensation system.'

The appraisal system did little to reinforce the important new issues of focus on continuous improvement and greater employee development. 'We really weren't helping our employees understand what they needed to do to perform more effectively.' This frustrated managers and employees alike. At the same time, there was evidence that appraisals across departments were not consistent . . . that different standards applied, depending on which department you were in.

After extensive consultations with its managers and other employees the company replaced this ineffective appraisal system with an on-going performance management process which included a definition of the behavioural characteristics of its top performers – on both the professional/technical level and the managerial level.

(This is a mixed model approach which is described in more detail in Chapter 8: Total Performance Management.)

A Regional Health Organisation in the United States faced similar problems with its appraisal system. A quality programme begun in 1987 had reoriented the hospital staff towards a greater customer/patient focus. Yet its appraisal system spent little time appraising how well its employees met customer expectations and more time on clinical/technical matters. The reviews were usually two-hour sessions at the end of the year, with nothing in between. Usually these kind of reviews only captured the last two months of activity (freshest in the mind of the manager), consequently a lot was stored up during the year that wasn't discussed appropriately.

The new performance management process that was developed for its 300-bed hospital was based on comments gathered from both patient and employees. The new process used Hay/McBer competencies to define the key customer expectations. ('As we developed each competency, if we couldn't link it back to the customer, we considered it a weak competency and threw it out.' HR director.) For managers and supervisors the company identified 23 core competencies ranging from communications to problem-solving to team leadership.

These competencies provided the foundation for a new on-going interactive process involving planning, coaching and review. In the new process managers and subordinates planned together; at least one formal coaching session was required during the year, but many formal and informal sessions occurred. The subsequent year-end review provided less of the often unpleasant surprises commonly associated with traditional performance appraisals.

In our third example, a chemical manufacturer decided to apply the principles of total quality management to its performance appraisal process. The TQM process had in its basis the management of processes to meet customer expectations 100 per cent of the time. Through its corporate commitment to total quality management it had developed a performance management process that addressed the expectations of one set of internal customers – their employees.

The existing performance appraisal process was not meeting customer expectations because:

- it was one-sided ('boss centred' not 'customer centred');
- it focused on individual performance (and unconsciously encouraged people to compete against one another);
- it was inflexible (and did not allow for the redefinition of objectives through the year);
- it was difficult to administer consistently across the company.

The outcome was that the traditional appraisal process was not effective at producing a quality product for the customers or the employee. Interestingly the employees said that they didn't want to get rid of performance appraisal; they wanted a more effective process which would meet their expectations more fully:

- They wanted to be assessed on their performance – a means of getting feedback so that they could continually improve in their jobs and grow in professional competence.
- They wanted to be recognised and rewarded for their accomplishments, held accountable for their actions and constructively supported if their work strayed off the desired target line.
- Furthermore they expected managers to create a working atmos-

phere where the values of fairness, truth-telling, promise-keeping and respect for the individual were paramount.

The new performance management process was based on the premise that the employee knows more or can learn better than anyone else – including the supervisor – about his or her own capabilities, developmental needs and personal goals. That is why the responsibility for performance, personal development and the achievement of full potential in current jobs was placed under the employee's own control. The process was employee-driven and bonded to the total quality management process. The supervisor became a coach and advisor helping to identify customers' needs, establish goals and develop plans to meet customer, department and company expectations.

For this company the performance management process became a dynamic process that met the expectations of its internal and external customers and contributed to the success of the organisation. Most importantly, it worked.

These three examples illustrate the direction in which performance management is moving. Many organisations are breaking away from the mechanistic framework imposed by traditional performance appraisal schemes. These changes, and there are many others – such as upwards appraisal, 360 degree feedback and self-managed performance – indicate the end of 'performance appraisal' as we know it.

Doubtless the idea of a universally applied, personnel-driven, standard procedure that stays rigidly in place, unchanged over years, will linger on in some organisations, but its days are numbered. In its place are a number of separate but linked processes, applied in different ways according to the needs of local circumstances. Appraisal, as we know it, has outlined its usefulness. It is time to get rid of it.

The next chapter describes the steps you can take to re-engineer your current appraisal process into a fully effective and dynamic performance management process.

Part 2

Re-engineering the Performance Management Process

Chapter 5

Re-engineering the Performance Management Process: A Summary

What can you do to re-engineer the performance management process? From wide experience we believe that there are seven key elements for an effective performance management process. These are summarised below:

An Integrated Management Process

Performance management should not be the once-a-year event – 'the annual ritual'. Truly effective performance management becomes part of everyday work life – 'the way we do things' – embracing the four phases of performance planning, managing, reviewing and recognition. You have to plan for performance, you have to decide how you are going to agree what you need to deliver, both in terms of the way you believe and the achievement of measurable objectives – that is performance planning.

You have to manage it, to monitor it, talk about it and develop for it – usually over a year – but even then it can be changed. You have to review it – but not through old-style performance appraisals. It is about jointly reviewing your progress and where you are going in the future. At the heart of it, because we are talking about positive performance improvement, it's a lot about recognition and reward – be it money, enhanced status or something else.

A Holistic Approach

The process should not be isolated within the organisation. It should be integrated into the way the performance of the business is managed and it should link with other key processes such as business strategy, employee development, and total quality management. You have to find ways to take the management and ownership performance into the heart of the way you do business – to drive the implementation of your business plans and strategies and to provide the processes and language you use for creating the future.

Total Performance Management

Traditional approaches to performance management focus only on the setting of job objectives. In other words, they defined the 'what' of performance. However, in the longer term substantial performance improvement is likely to happen only if employees have an understanding of the key competencies which are associated with superior performance. The 'mixed model' approach defines the 'how' of performance, not just the 'what'. A competency-based approach focuses not simply on standards to do the job adequately, but shifts the emphasis to how people can deliver their best performance. It also helps people look at what they can do to improve, by giving models of superior behaviour which people can see and understand.

Fit with Work Cultures

Organisations differ not only in terms of their shapes and sizes: their cultures are different too. Cultures define the kinds of behaviours, values and processes which govern how the organisation operates. Many organisations are realising that they should 'fit' their performance management processes to their work cultures. Different organisations with different cultures need to do things differently and they need different competencies to manage this and deliver performance improvement. So it is critical to know what kind of culture(s) you have, through a diagnostic survey, and then to design the performance management process which provides the best fit.

Self-Managed Individuals and Teams

Chapter 3 (The Changing Shape of Organisations) describes how organisations are getting 'flatter' and more flexibly structured. Many are moving away from a command and control way of operating to a style which is more empowering, placing greater responsibility on individuals and teams. In these circumstances it is essential to create an 'empowering' climate in which individuals and teams take on greater ownership of the performance management process. This requires development and training to help managers and other employees learn these new ways of managing. We have to accept that many managers will find little time to manage the performance of others throughout the year. A growing emphasis on self-management will help to bridge this gap as long as it does not signal to managers that it is acceptable for them to abdicate totally from their responsibilities to manage others.

Effective Links with Rewards

In our employee attitude surveys, many employees thought that there were poor links between performance management and the reward system – they do not see a real link between what they agree to do and what they get paid, either in pay increases or bonuses. The sum of all this is that the motivational value they get for the effort they put in over the year is just not enough.

The reward system must reinforce the kinds of behaviours which are central in the performance management process. It is not just about the size of rewards, it is about fit, ie feeling that there is proper recognition given within the working environment.

A Motivating Work Climate

A well designed performance management process is a prerequisite for having an effective process, but it is not sufficient. The process will only be effective if it is taking place in a motivating work climate. This is created primarily by the use of supportive managerial styles – predominantly authoritative and coaching. These have often been underdeveloped in previous appraisal processes. Managers have got to see themselves as enablers rather than controllers. They add value by creating supportive work climates in which their staff feel motivated and will give the discretionary effort required for superior performance. They will need the confidence to manage that role rather than trying to lead from the front all of the time. The effective performance management process will have a positive impact on the work climate – by giving greater clarity and responsibility to employees, better feedback and recognition for their achievements.

The seven factors mentioned above are the key elements of a re-engineered performance management process. What we are really talking about is a better way of managing, something that you do most of the time, that fits in with other processes in the organisation and which, ultimately, leads to improved organisational improvement. The process will help all employees see where they are going and where their contribution fits in with where the organisation is going. It will be a process which is valued and something which will lever the performance of the organisation.

The remaining chapters describe in detail these key elements. If you work through each element you will have a better chance of creating the kind of performance management process which is more purposeful, better at motivating people and able to respond more creatively to the challenges ahead. Then to make it happen you need to invest in the development and training to help managers learn new ways of managing and you need to allow adequate time to develop and put the new processes in place.

Chapter 6

An Integrated Management Process

THE ELEMENTS OF AN EFFECTIVE PERFORMANCE MANAGEMENT PROCESS

In the first stage of the Institute of Personnel Management research project[1] into performance management, Stephen Bevan and Marc Thompson of the Institute of Manpower Studies came to the conclusion that a 'textbook' performance management process exhibits the following features.

The organisation:

- has a shared vision of its objectives or a mission statement, which it communicates to all its employees;
- sets individual performance management targets which are related both to business needs and wider organisational objectives;
- conducts regular, formal reviews of progress towards these targets;
- uses the review process to identify training, development and reward outcomes;

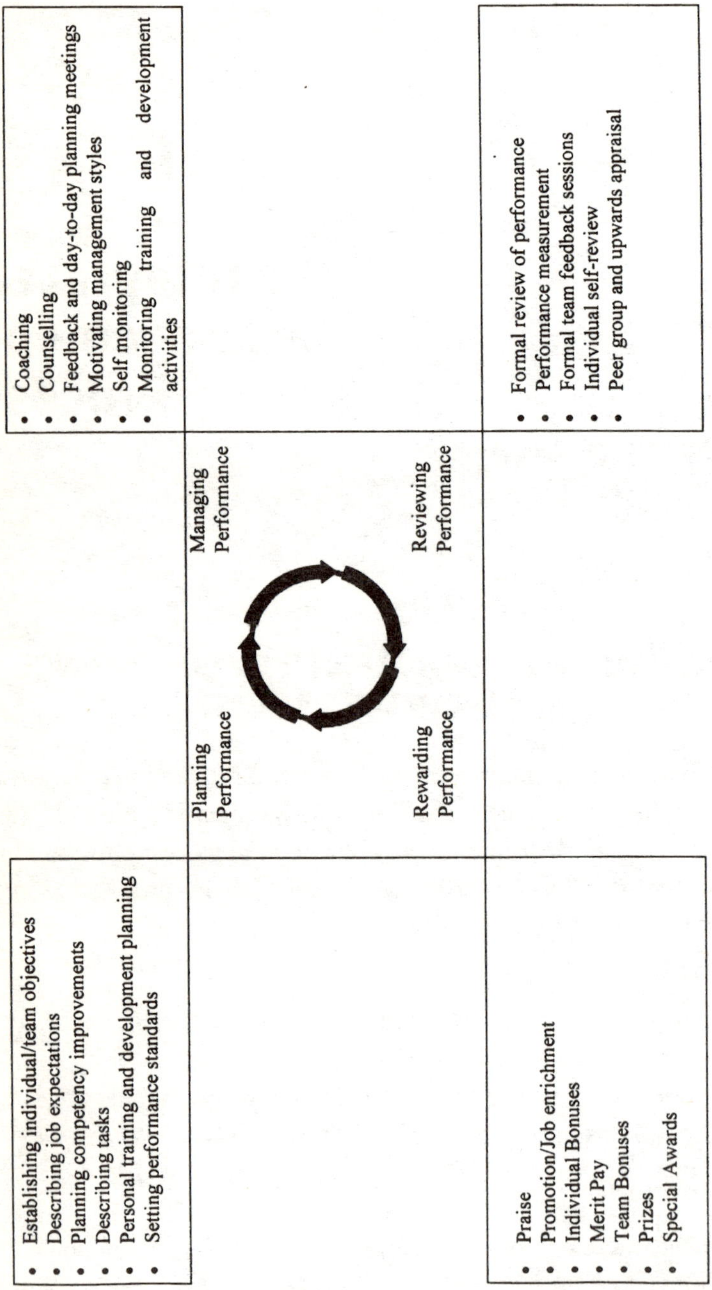

- Establishing individual/team objectives
- Describing job expectations
- Planning competency improvements
- Describing tasks
- Personal training and development planning
- Setting performance standards

- Coaching
- Counselling
- Feedback and day-to-day planning meetings
- Motivating management styles
- Self monitoring
- Monitoring training and development activities

Planning Performance

Managing Performance

Rewarding Performance

Reviewing Performance

- Praise
- Promotion/Job enrichment
- Individual Bonuses
- Merit Pay
- Team Bonuses
- Prizes
- Special Awards

- Formal review of performance
- Performance measurement
- Formal team feedback sessions
- Individual self-review
- Peer group and upwards appraisal

Figure 6.1. *Performance management processes need to contain all these elements*

- ❑ evaluates the effectiveness of the whole process and its contribution to overall performance to allow changes and improvements to be made.

Bevan and Thompson suggested that this textbook approach placed too much emphasis on a top-down approach and underplayed the extent to which training and development and reward systems should be driven from bottom up.

Performance management: an integrated management process

An integrated performance management process should be designed to encourage open, ongoing communication between the manager and the employee about performance issues. It should be seen as a flexible process which involves managers and their staff as partners, but within a framework which sets out how they can best work together. The framework should reduce the degree to which the process is a top-down process by giving more scope for employees to manage themselves and by encouraging a freer upwardly managed approach.

THE KEY PHASES OF EFFECTIVE PERFORMANCE MANAGEMENT

Effective performance management has four basic phases: planning, managing, reviewing and rewarding performance. Figure 6.1 shows the content of each phase and how they shape up as a year-long process. It is a continuous cycle, with employees and managers working together to establish key objectives, monitor progress towards these objectives, assess results and provide reward/recognition for achievements.

1. Performance planning

This is the process of identifying the desired performance and gaining employees' commitment to perform to those expectations. It is of vital importance because unless individuals know what is expected of them in the future they will be unable to work effectively to achieve the objectives. Corporate performance is generally described in terms of results: short- and long-term profits, dividends, return on assets and return on investments. Similarly performance planning focuses on individual/team results: what an individual achieves and, perhaps just as important, how these results are achieved.

Performance planning that clearly identifies the expected results, as well as the behaviours and skills the individual is expected to demonstrate, provides a specific action plan aimed at a clear target. A planning strategy that solicits the active participation of employees in the process will help to build commitment to the achievement of the objectives.

Therefore a core part of good performance management is to ensure that managers and their staff develop the clearest possible picture of the key priorities among a multitude of tasks that face them every day. Without this, many individuals will be overwhelmed by the conflicting demands on their time, and as a result may simply not make the right decisions. With clarity of understanding, good performance is possible.

The critical, and often most difficult, part of performance management is to define clearly what 'good' or 'excellent' performance looks like. For some individuals, describing what success in their job looks like, and what they need to do to achieve it, is more difficult than may first appear.

Figure 6.2 describes how for different jobs in the organisation the focus of performance management may vary between three types of measures.

- **Output targets**: 'hard' measurable output targets often derived from accountability/key result area statements.
- **Competencies**: the display of certain behaviours (eg initiative, achievement orientation) which are associated with superior performance in the job.
- **Tasks**: the completion of certain predetermined tasks to the required standard.

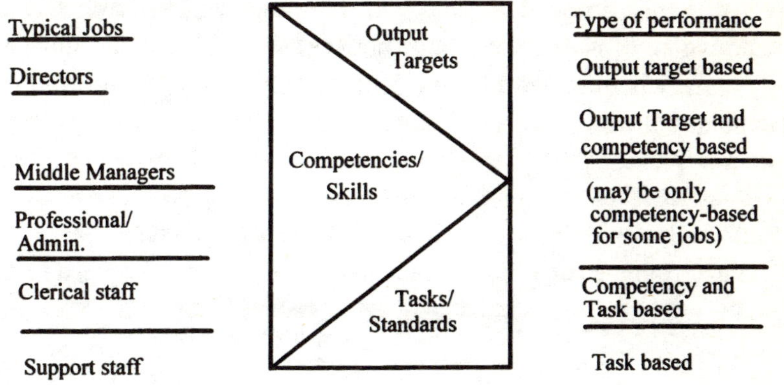

Figure 6.2 *Focus for performance improvement*

The Planning Phase: Key Processes

Establishing team/individual objectives: The definition of team/individual objectives is an important element in performance management. Business unit objectives are normally set through the business strategy, planning and budgeting processes for the year (or longer). Individual/team objectives may be set through:

- establishing improvements over previous years;
- external bodies that set targets and standards to be achieved;
- benchmarking – internal setting of standards and targets compared with the best in the field.

Normally the setting of team objectives is the responsibility of managers, but consulting their staff can usually add to clarity. It is important to remember that the team planning meetings decide not only what the team plans to achieve, and who is accountable for what, but also identifies what will not be done or achieved. Establishing team/individual objectives sets priorities.

Describing the job roles of individuals: Defining individual roles and performance expectations is a key to sound performance planning. A good mechanism you can use for this purpose is the language of 'key accountabilities'. A key accountability is simply an area of responsibility for which the job holder is expected to produce results. Most jobs will have between 4–8 key accountabilities; an example is illustrated below. Defining job roles can be done by the manager, the team or the individuals themselves but it is an essential prerequisite to the performance planning phase.

Key Accountabilities – Manufacturing Manager (Healthcare Products)

Purpose: to manage the production of speciality healthcare products.
Key Accountabilities:

1. Oversee the deployment and day to day direction of production staff.
2. Operate to budgets, in line with demand.
3. Meet target dates for introduction of new products, line extensions and promotions.
4. Ensure the development of key subordinates.
5. Closely liaise with Planning, Marketing, Technical, Engineering and Finance personnel to ensure new products and plans are met.
6. Meet profit improvement targets.

Increasingly organisations are defining jobs not only in terms of key accountabilities, but also of the skills and competencies necessary for success. These are often called *role profiles*.

A role profile

This approach is illustrated below with an example of a project manager in a public health education organisation in the United Kingdom.

Project Manager: Role Profile (Level 12)		
Key Accountabilities	Skills	Competencies
1. Direct cluster of large projects. 2. Secure appropriate resources for projects. 3. Ensures projects deliver on time and at required quality.	Project planning. Knowledge of specialist areas covered. Resource negotiation. Budget control accounting.	Concern for quality 4. Expertise 4. Networking 3. Influence and impact 4. Planning and organising 5.
4. Makes contribution to strategic direction of organisation.	Understanding company strategy.	Communication 6. Interpersonal understanding 4.
5. Fosters good team climate in large teams.	People management.	Teamwork 4. Developing others 4.

The advantage of this approach is that the 'job worth' and the 'person worth' of the jobs can be defined.

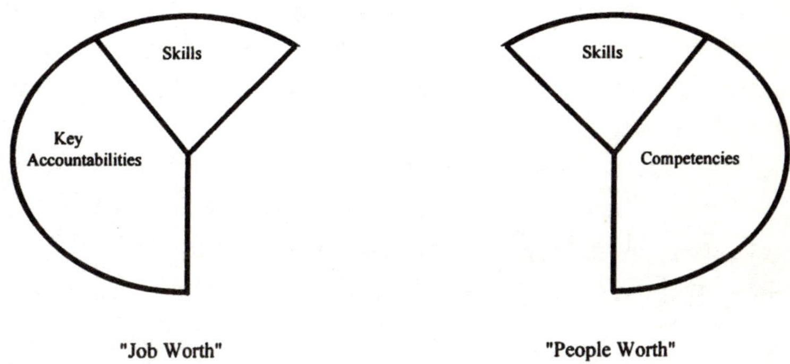

Objective setting: A key part of performance management is the setting and agrceing of team/individual objectives. They highlight, for the team and the individual, the clarity of understanding of their jobs, and provide a focus to their actions and behaviours in the coming period.

As Williams[2] has written:

> The setting of objectives is the management process which ensures that every individual employee knows what role they need to play and what results they need to achieve to maximise their contribution to the overall business.

In essence it enables employees to know what is required of them and on what basis their performance and contribution will be assessed.

Also Williams suggests that objectives should:

- ❑ be jointly agreed by manager and individual as both realistic and challenging and, as such, they are 'owned';
- ❑ measure the actual level of achievement so that the basis on which performance is assessed can be understood in advance and is as clear as possible;
- ❑ support the overall business strategies of the company.

Other criteria which need to bc satisfied are:

- ❑ the objectives should be appropriate to improving the performance of the individual concerned, and be capable of influence or control of that person;
- ❑ ideally objectives should involve some degree of stretch for the individual. Objectives that are too easy, or too difficult, will not motivate individual performance improvement;
- ❑ when objectives are set they should be capable of on-going monitoring as well as end of year assessment.

Possible objectives for the manufacturing manager whose accountabilities were described earlier are shown below:

Manufacturing Manager – Healthcare Products Company

Objectives:

1. Keep manufacturing operating budget in line with demand to year-end savings target of £25k.
2. Establish (at least) monthly meetings with sales team to exchange information and match product mix more closely to customer requirements.
3. Restructure manufacturing cells and reorganise Personnel. Reduce headcount by two by September 1993.
4. Put forward proposal for development of new mixing area by end of Q.2.

Development Planning: Clarifying the job roles, responsibilities and objectives is a way of defining what the job holder has to do. However, it is important to realise that each job holder, regardless of current levels of performance, can achieve better results if personal performance improvement objectives are built into the planning process. This focuses on how they achieve their objectives, what they can do themselves to develop better performance and any support that is available from the organisation to help them.

The development plan will be more effective if it meets these conditions:

- ❑ Agreeing personal development objectives should be an interactive process between managers and their staff.
- ❑ Individuals should be encouraged to own and take responsibility for their own development.
- ❑ The discussion should focus on future performance, rather than past 'failings'.
- ❑ Training and development activities should support the achievement of key objectives identified during the planning phase.
- ❑ The development activities should fit the preferred learning style of the individual. Thus there should be a variety of development activities. For example, formal training courses and reading, use of learning resource centres, project work.

2. Managing performance

This is the on-going process of working towards the performance expectations established in the planning phase. It is probably the most neglected area of the performance management cycle. Together, manager and employee review the employee's performance on a periodic basis. If it is on track, or exceeding expectations, the manager provides positive reinforcement to keep performance at a high level. If performance is below expectations, the manager coaches the employee on improving the trouble spots. This involves developing strategies with the employee to determine appropriate action plans.

Managing performance involves several activities.

Coaching

This involves working with an individual on a specific task of activity that forms part of their job, in a planned manner so that their knowledge, competence or skill is improved. Coaching on a timely basis eliminates the often unpleasant – punitive – 'post-mortem' aspects of the performance appraisal.

So what are the essential ingredients of 'good' coaching?

- ❑ Coaching is a learning process, not a teaching process.
- ❑ The individuals are responsible for planning and achieving the task, but are supported, counselled and monitored by their managers throughout the learning process.
- ❑ Feedback should be specific, timely and focused on positive achievements as well as the need to improve some aspects of performance.

Managers who periodically track and review performance let employees know where they stand; performance appraisal discussions hold no surprises. Instead manager and team member discuss good or bad aspects of performance when they actually occur – the best time to modify behaviour. The year-end performance review becomes a summary with little or no new information, and discussion focuses on planning for the future performance cycle.

Counselling

Effective counselling is an important part of managing performance. This is necessary when, for whatever reason, performance has not reached up to expectations and the manager needs to take a formal and planned approach in order to help the job holder overcome the obstacles. This is not a disciplinary measure – it is meant to be positive and helpful. So how do you do it?

- ❑ The sessions should be timely. That is, they should occur soon after the problems arise. Do not delay your counselling sessions until the end of year.
- ❑ They should be planned in advance and, as for formal review meetings, should be in an undisturbed and comfortable environment. It would be helpful if at the meeting both manager and job holder have any facts or examples which are relevant to the issues.
- ❑ There should be a two-way dialogue. In most situations it will be more constructive if the manager is in 'active listening' mode. A two-way session will encourage, and demonstrate, openness.
- ❑ Do not focus only on negative issues. To maintain a good climate it is also important to be factual and specific about positive aspects of performance. There should be positive reinforcement as well as specific advice on how to improve some aspects of performance.
- ❑ Always end with agreement on specific action plans which both parties are committed to take to bring about performance improvements.

On-going Progress Reviews

Performance management should be a line management process, not a once-a-year review meeting. Therefore it is essential to integrate the process with your normal business planning/work activities. It means becoming more focused on the links between individuals' capabilities, objectives and output and the overall success of the organisation.

If the individual/team objectives are critical to the success of the organisation they need to be monitored on a regular and routine process. They are too important to be left alone for the best part of a year. For some jobs a discussion and summary of progress every three months may be sensible. For other short cycle jobs or when the person is a new employee, or in a new role, weekly or daily feedback may be appropriate. Here are some pointers to effective progress reviews:

- ❑ Fit the progress reviews around the business cycles and individuals in the job.
- ❑ Plan progress reviews into work schedules.
- ❑ Do not squeeze them out by pressure of other work. On-going review of progress *is* a part of managers'/job holders' accountabilities.
- ❑ Keep them informal and focused. They are not formal or final reviews of performance. They are for information-gathering, information-sharing and agreeing actions to keep progress on track.
- ❑ If circumstances dictate, change the objectives.
- ❑ Record progress to date and agreed actions but do not be overwhelmed by paper. A simple record will suffice, as shown below.

Objectives	Progress (+/=/?)	Actions
1.		
2.		
3.		
4.		
5.		

\+ = beyond expectations
= = meeting expectations
? = below expectations

Self-Monitoring

An effective performance management process has to be a partnership between manager and employee. As organisations get flatter and encourage 'self-managed' processes, it is essential for all individuals to own the performance management process – it should not be left solely to the manager to maintain the process. The individual job holder is a key stakeholder in performance management and should be encouraged to recognise the benefits of actively managing and taking responsibility for their own performance.

They should be encouraged to:

- seek specific guidance/feedback from colleagues/peers who have a view on their daily performance;
- participate fully in discussions about their performance;
- review their own performance and form a judgement about how well they have done prior to any performance reviews;
- monitor the management information the manager is using to judge performance.

3. Performance review

Performance review provides the opportunity to step back from day-to-day activities, assess performance trends and plan for the future. Because periodic performance reviews have essentially eliminated any surprises, both manager and job holder can anticipate the nature of the discussion and prepare for the meeting accordingly. Career development, a natural outgrowth of this discussion, helps build the employee's commitment and loyalty to the organisation, increasing motivation and productivity as well.

The formal review

The formal performance review is both the beginning and the end point of the annual process. The analysis of past performance provides the basis for planning next year's expectations, and at the same time, it 'closes the loop' of the current cycle. Formal review describes an event, often annual, in which the manager and job holder form an agreed view on the job holder's performance in the preceding year. This part is synonymous with 'performance appraisal' and for many job holders their experiences have not been happy ones.

> We found that appraisals too often were one-sided [manager to job holder] and that managers disliked doing them.
>
> Senior Vice President Human Resources
> US Financial Institution

> It leaves people bitter, crushed, bruised, battered, desolate, despondent, dejected, feeling inferior, some even depressed, unfit to work for weeks after the receipt of a rating...
>
> W Edwards Deming, *Out of a Crisis,* MIT Press, 1982

So what do you have to do in order to create a more positive and helpful performance review?

1. Link the reviews to the planning process. You should review the agreed key objectives as well as whole job performance during the preceding twelve month period.
2. Meetings should be planned in advance and dates/times/location agreed with the job holder.
3. All information on the job holder's performance should be shared with the job holder, preferably in advance of the meeting.
4. The review should focus on performance only; it should not be concerned with other elements which do not genuinely link with performance, eg behaviour traits, issues of gender or race.
5. Both parties should prepare adequately for the meeting. It may be sensible to consult with colleagues who work with the appraisee.
6. If periodic progress reviews have taken place throughout the year, there should be 'no surprises' and relatively little anxiety about the meeting in that such meetings have become a regular part of 'managing'.

7. If a rating system is used, staff should be clear about the significance of different ratings and what standards apply to each. Consistency matters a lot and the organisation should have a monitoring system to ensure that there is consistency between departments as well as between individual appraisers.
8. If performance ratings affect salary, the organisation must decide how the links are to be made, the timing of pay increases and should communicate the results of the pay link separate from the review. Performance-related pay should not be the driver of the performance management process. It is not usual, nor sensible, to discuss pay in the same meetings as performance review.
9. Both appraiser and appraisee should agree (or agree to disagree) a written record of the meeting.
10. Some organisations have a 'grand parent' to sign off the record of the meeting. This is felt to increase the probability of reaching greater consistency and objectivity. Usually it is the line manager's manager.

Individual Self-Review

All individual job holders should be partners in the performance management. Usually they will have an accurate picture of their own performance. They certainly will have an opinion about how well they have done. Therefore they should be encouraged to participate fully in reviewing their achievements, and understanding the factors that have led to successful performance in some aspects of their job or problems in other areas.

In the United Kingdom a teacher appraisal scheme of a local authority presents a prompt sheet on which appraisees should rate themselves. The teacher's contribution is divided into seven areas: Planning; Organisational Skills; Follow-up Skills; Communication Skills; Fostering Teamwork; Relationships with People and Professional Development. Figure 6.3 is a prompt sheet for fostering teamwork.

	Experienced in/happy with	Keeping my eye on this	Need to spend more time on this	Not relevant/ not of immediate concern
Being member of/helping to foster an enthusiastic and productive group				
Involving people in decision-making/ identifying goals to gain their commitment				
Developing individuals to their full potential				
Developing self-discipline in a group and their ability to solve problems				
Successfully facing up to and dealing with conflict				
Accepting the responsibility to take initiatives/make decisions.				

Figure 6.3 *Fostering teamwork*

In another organisation, each job holder is asked to think through their responses to these questions, prior to the performance review discussion:

1. What critical abilities does my job require? To what extent do I fulfil them?
2. What do I like best about my job? Least?
3. What were my specific accomplishments during this appraisal period?
4. Which goals or standards did I fall short of meeting?
5. How could my supervisor help me do a better job?
6. Is there anything that the organisation or my supervisor does that hinders my effectiveness?
7. What changes would improve my performance?
8. Does my present job make the best use of my capabilities? How could I become more productive?
9. Do I need more experience or training in any aspect of my current job? How could it be accomplished?
10. What have I done since my last appraisal to prepare myself for more responsibility?
11. What new goals and standards should be established for the next appraisal period? Which old ones need to be modified or deleted?
12. What do I expect to be doing five years from now?

Peer Groups and Upward Appraisal

In recent years some organisations have been trying to break the 'top down' approach which is synonymous with traditional performance appraisal approaches. The concept of 360° feedback has emerged, ie getting feedback from manager, subordinates and peers.

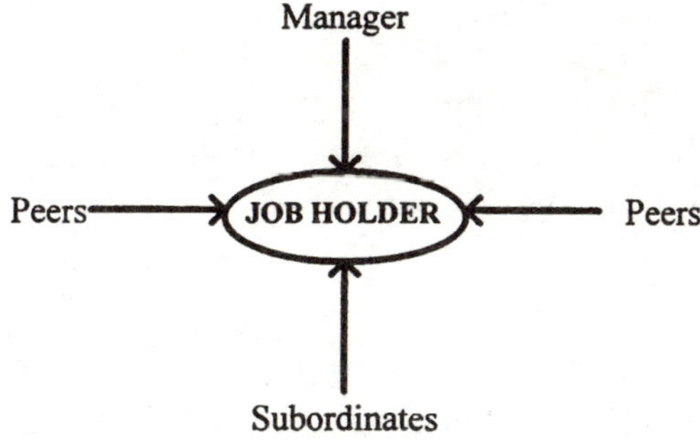

In a UK Health Education organisation, five people contribute towards the appraisal of the skills/competencies of a colleague. These five people are agreed between the manager and job holder in advance of the meeting. They should be people with whom the job holder has worked closely and who are able to form a view about his/her competencies. Ideally, they should include individuals who are 'up', 'down' and 'across' the organisation in relation to the person being assessed. Each person is sent a copy of a competency rating questionnaire for completion. The job holder also completes a self-assessment questionnaire. The results are summarised on a competency rating record sheet:

Competency	**Rating**: Write down the level at which each person rated the individual						Overall rating
Teamworking	SELF 2	MANAGER 2	3	2	2	1	2
Communication	SELF 4	MANAGER 3	4	4	2	2	4

The competency rating is focused on 4–6 key competencies only, and is a part of a wider performance review process which also includes performance against objectives. Clearly this is a fairly complex process but it reflects this organisation's evolution into a competency-based matrix structure in which individuals take on flexible roles with a variety of project teams throughout the year.

To set up peer group or upward appraisal the following factors are important considerations:

- Careful thought should go into choosing the contributors and the form of feedback. People who have axes to grind, who have particular prejudices or who are close friends seldom view performance dispassionately.
- The idea may be uncomfortable to all parties concerned. It needs careful planning, communication and implementation.
- Appraisal judgements should be based on evidence of specific behaviours throughout the year. This evidence should be quoted

by each appraiser for each judgement.

❑ All information from other sources should be available to the appraisee and attributable in origin. All comments, and supporting evidence, should be written down.

Examples of feedback forms are shown in Figure 6.4.

Upwards Appraisal Form (The Johari Form)

Circle the score which best represents your opinions of your manager, where
1 = very poor and 5 = excellent.

Demonstrates leadership	1	2	3	4	5
Always serves the customer	1	2	3	4	5
Develops and trains employees	1	2	3	4	5
Is decisive	1	2	3	4	5

TO: (Name) . . . .

I am collecting data on other people's perception of me. This will help me in understanding myself and where I can develop. I would be grateful for your help in answering the questions below and returning to me.

1. What is the most important aspect of my behaviour as a manager which you value?
2. What is the single most important thing you would like to see me change to improve my effectiveness as a manager?

Figure 6.4 *Appraisal feedback form*

If all subordinates rate their managers, through upwards appraisal, statistically the ratings will be more reliable than the traditional 'top down' approach. The more subordinates the better. However, upwards appraisal will incur greater cost since more forms have to be processed and clearly is more time consuming. Subordinates will need training on how to rate individuals without falling into some of the well-known traps of traditional 'appraisals'. Obviously upwards appraisal will work only in work climates which foster openness, trust and honesty.

Rewarding Performance

Reward is an important part of the 'feedback loop' in performance management. However, it is not necessarily only concerned with money. A reward only has a positive effect on the individual if it is:

- valued by them;
- appropriate to the effort put in and the achievement.

Since each individual might be motivated by different things, an effective performance reward process should be sufficiently flexible to cater for individual needs. Consequently, there is a wide range of types of reward:

Praise
Promotion
Individual Bonuses
Merit Pay
Team Bonuses
Prizes
Special Awards

These are discussed in greater detail in Chapter 12 (Effective Links with Rewards).

SUMMARY

Performance management should be designed as an integrated core management process which becomes 'the way we do things'. It should embrace four key phases – planning; managing; reviewing and rewarding. If your approach to managing performance resembles this model you will have begun to move a long way from the one-dimensional model of traditional performance appraisal. The next chapter shows how your performance management process should be a major agent for organisational change.

References

1. Institute of Personnel Management (1992) *Performance Management in the UK – An analysis of the issues* IPM, London
2. Williams, S (1991) *Strategy and Objectives* (in the *Handbook of Performance Management*) (ed. F Leale), IPM, London

Chapter 7

A Holistic Approach

AN INTEGRATED APPROACH TO HUMAN RESOURCE MANAGEMENT

Many initiatives on human resource management fail to achieve their objectives for one simple reason – they have not been integrated with other initiatives and processes within the organisation. Because of this lack of integration, the initiatives are often regarded by managers as irrelevant (to the real business) or inconsistent with other initiatives.

Let us illustrate this point by reference to initiatives which have gone wrong:

- ***Lack of strategic relevance***: An appraisal scheme based on long-term individual development was introduced at a time when the business was facing short-term operating difficulties. Managers paid lip service to the scheme but focused their attention elsewhere because they did not see the strategic relevance of the initiative. The result was disillusionment and lack of commitment, and the failure of a constructive idea.
- ***Unprepared middle managers***: The company introduced wide

salary bands to permit scope for flexible progression of individuals according to demonstrated competency, so that high performers could be directly recognised. The original concern here was that managers would lose control of consistency and cost: in fact, salary budgets were underspent as managers who were previously used to rigid frameworks erred on the side of caution in difficult economic conditions. The result was frustrated managers and staff. The managers had not been sufficiently prepared for the new tasks and consequently they stuck to their old ways.

- ***Lack of consistency with other initiatives***: A job evaluation process was introduced based on comprehensive job descriptions at a time when a number of project-based areas were consciously adopting a more flexible team-based approach. The two initiatives appeared to many managers to send conflicting messages resulting in their discomfort and rejection of a fundamentally equitable initiative.

Such problems are quite common. Also they are avoidable. All major initiatives in human resource management need to be coordinated and should send the same messages. Your human resource programmes need to set an integrated overall approach to managing your people resources. A framework which many organisations find useful to understand and evaluate their human resource practices and programmes is Hay's Five Circle Model, shown in Figure 7.1.

Policy and practice need to be made explicit in the five key areas:

1. ***How organisations are shaped***: defining the structures, processes and values required by the organisation.
2. ***How work is valued***: establishing measurement criteria and tools to determine internal relativities within an organisation. This covers both job evaluation methodologies and innovative approaches using skill and competency frameworks.
3. ***How people are selected, motivated and developed***: defining the skills and competencies that are necessary for superior performance, using them in assessment and development programmes to create a motivating climate.

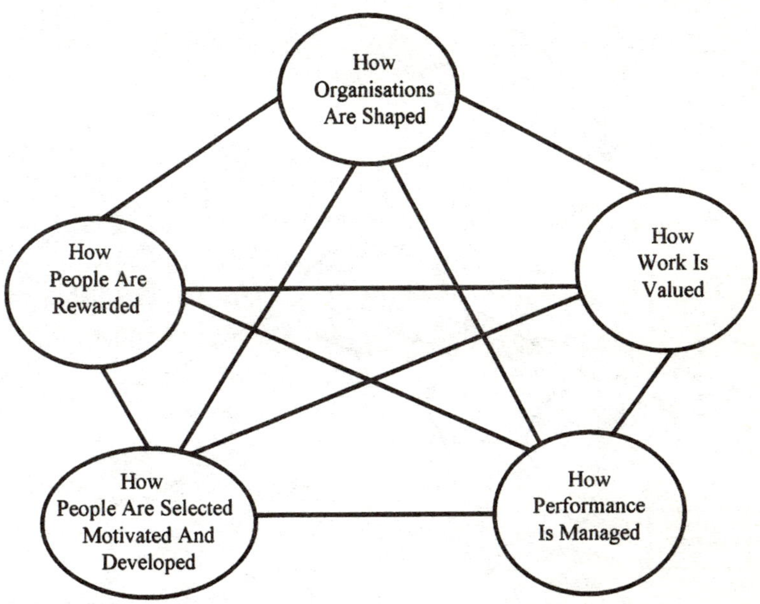

Figure 7.1 *The five circles of human resource management*

4. ***How people are rewarded***: ensuring that the total reward mix – base salaries, incentives, benefits and conditions of service – reinforces the organisation's purpose and that individuals are rewarded in ways which send clear and consistent messages about the organisation's values and priorities.
5. ***How performance is managed***: developing and implementing the processes which organisations use to link individual and team behaviour and activity to corporate requirements.

Initiatives which are adopted in any circle need to be evaluated against these criteria:

- ❑ Do they align with the business strategy?
- ❑ Do they support current or proposed initiatives in the other circles?

The five circle model is a useful diagnostic tool and illustrates how you can take an integrated approach to human resource management. Figures 7.2 and 7.3 show how this model was applied to a

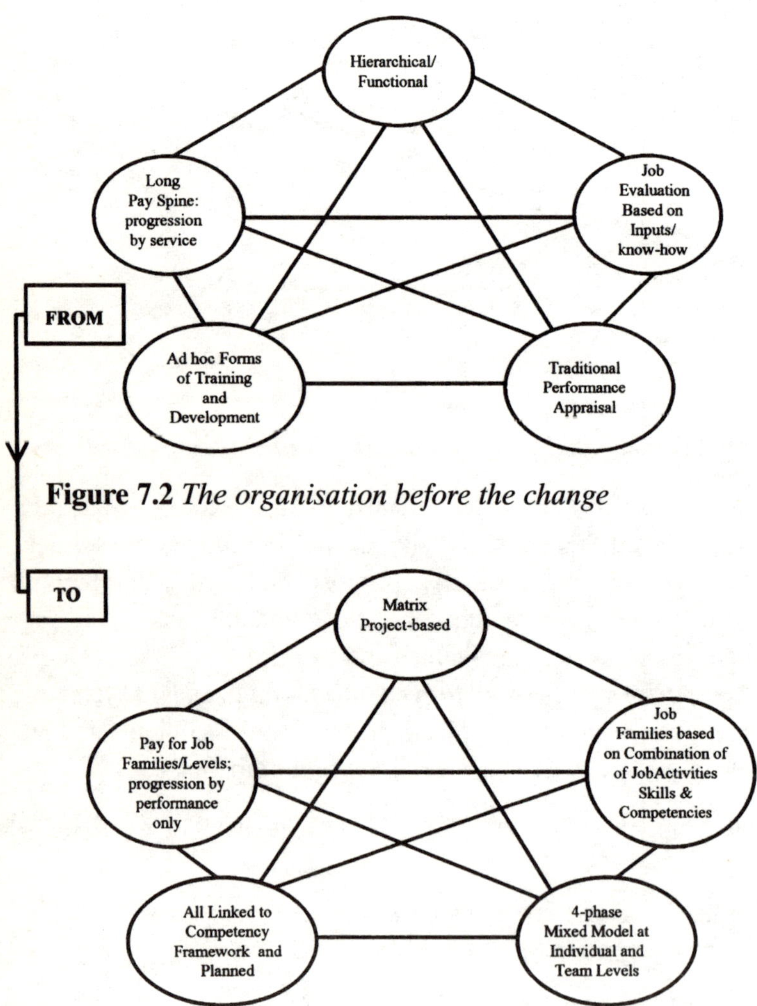

Figure 7.2 *The organisation before the change*

Figure 7.3 *The organisation after the change*

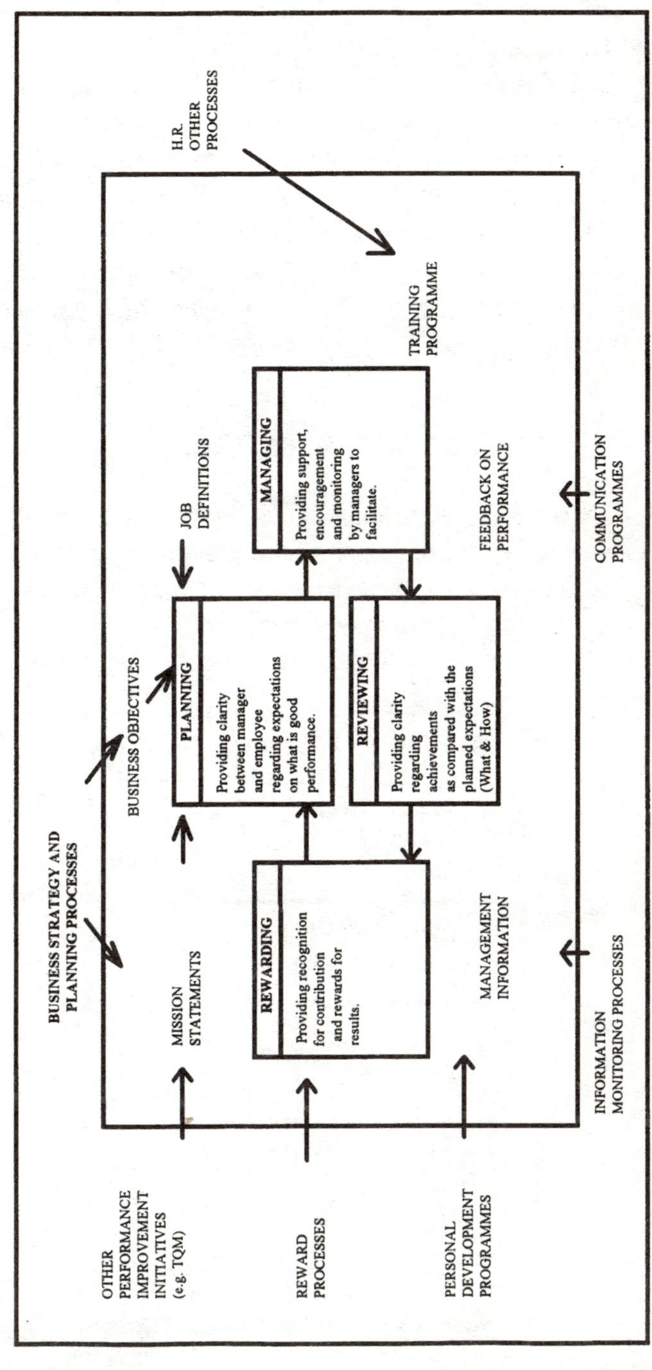

Figure 7.4 *A holistic approach to performance management*

change programme within a public health education organisation in the United Kingdom.

One of the major problems associated with the traditional performance appraisal approach is that it is too often treated as a 'stand alone' process – seemingly divorced from other internal processes and frequently regarded as marginalised within the organisation. This is a great pity and a lost opportunity. If the performance management process is well positioned it can be a powerful and valuable integrating process. It can be a key agent of organisational change.

A HOLISTIC APPROACH

Figure 7.4 shows a model of how performance management links with other management processes. There are a number of processes that are best integrated with performance management, which are set out below.

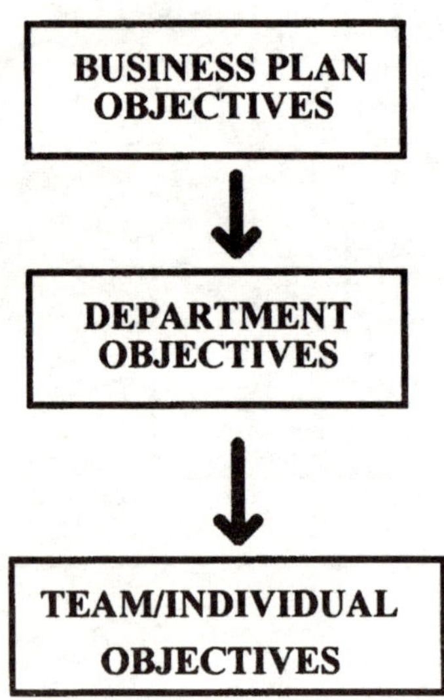

Figure 7.5 *Setting objectives throughout the organisation*

The Business Planning Process

Performance management is described as 'a process that sets out to link people and jobs at every level to the strategy and objectives of the organisation'. However, making it happen is not that easy.

Objectives agreed in the business plan have to be the key starting point for defining departmental/team/individual objectives. Having clarity about where the organisation is going and what teams/individuals have to do to achieve these organisational objectives is a key element in performance planning.

By linking the two processes together the performance management process can ensure that organisational objectives are cascaded down through the organisation (see Figure 7.5).

It is essential to ensure that horizontal communication takes place too. Frequently performance objectives are not achieved because of the failure to secure the support of colleagues/peers in other departments. A useful 'tool' to use in the performance planning phase is the inter-accountability matrix (Figure 7.6).

This process can be used at all levels in the organisation. Essentially it is about ensuring that team members are absolutely clear about what they are trying to achieve and who does what, ie who is accountable for delivering each agreed objective. Figure 7.6 shows the final set of collective agreements within the senior management team of a chemical manufacturing company. The business targets represent some of the key priorities for the business year – there were a total of 13 (from a list which was originally much higher). The symbols shown against each manager (P or S) show the type of accountability. For example, 'A' has a P against Target 6 (Quality). This means that he has prime accountability for delivering that objective and should receive support (S) from a number of colleagues. It should be said that the targets have been previously written out in specific and measurable terms. This exercise is essential for effective business planning. It is essential to start the process with the senior management team. Then it should be cascaded through the organisation – each senior manager can do the exercise with his/her team (see Figure 7.7).

Z FERTILISER CO									
A Business Targets / Senior Jobs Matrix									
TARGETS \ MANAGERS	A	B	C	D	E	F	G	H	I
1. Net Trading Profit	P	(P-Fe)	(P-Co_2)		S	S	S	S	S
2. Sales		S-Fe	P-Co_2)		S-Fe		P-Fe		
3. Manufacturing / Marketing		S	S ⟨ Fe / Co_2		S	P	S	S	P (a/h)
4. Safety	S	S	S	S	S	P	S	S	P (a/h)
5. ISO 9000		S	S	S	S	P (s/s)	S		P (a/h)
6. Quality	P	S	S		S	S	S	S	S
7. Achievement Culture	P	S	S	S	S	S	S	S	S

Figure 7.6 *An inter-accountability matrix in a chemical manufacturing company*

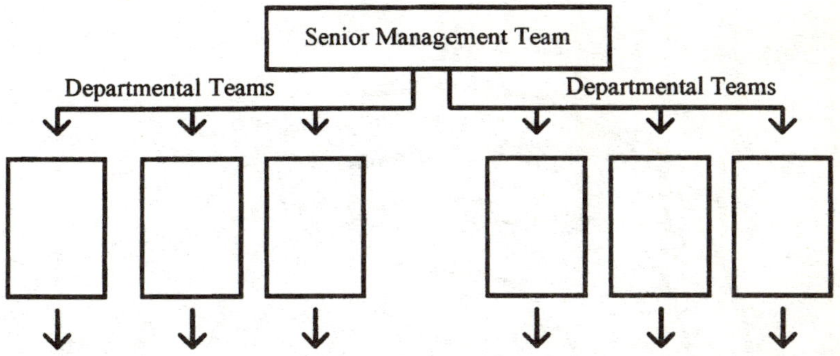

Figure 7.7 *Cascading the business plan*

In order to make effective links between business planning and performance management, it is vital that their 'cycles' are synchronised. The business planning cycle should precede the performance planning phase so that team/individual objectives can be set which are aligned to the company objectives and the performance management process can be focused primarily on the delivery of the company objectives.

Undoubtedly establishing a strong link between the processes for business planning and performance management should be a high priority for two reasons. Firstly, it is vital for the success of the organisation that there is a working process for delivering the key business objectives. Performance management can do this very well. Secondly, if the performance management process is seen to be about clarifying, communicating and ensuring action on the key business objectives, it raises its profile and perceived importance within the company. Effective performance management should be the major driver towards achieving success for the company by 'giving everyone a part of the strategic action'.

Figure 7.8 is one example from a major clearing bank of how different cycles are synchronised.

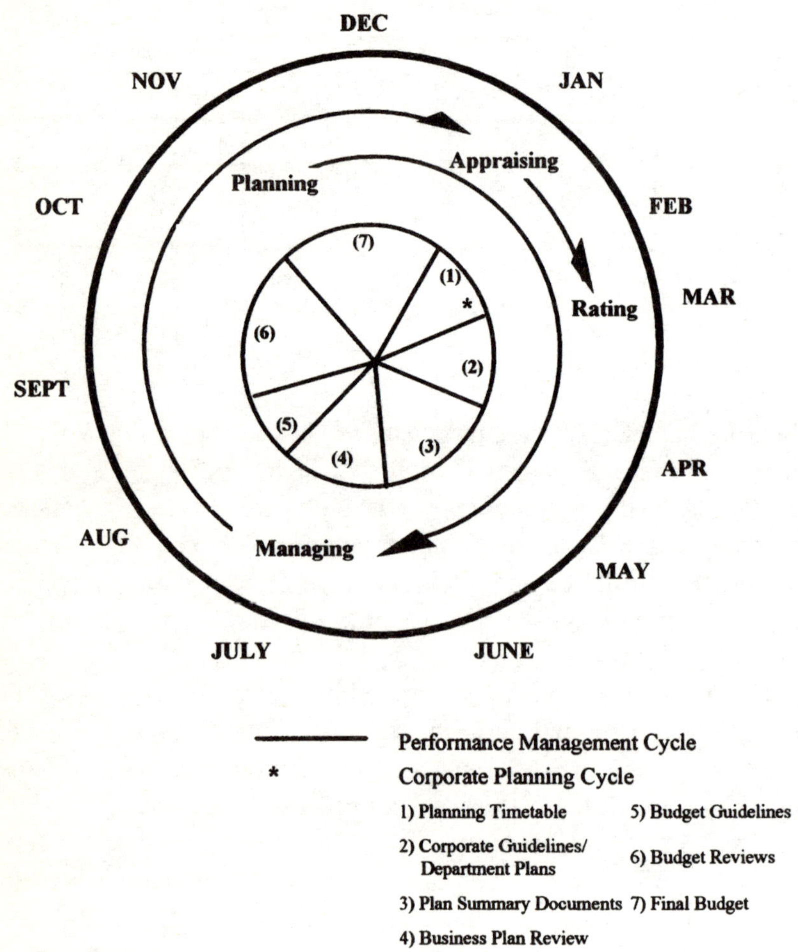

Figure 7.8 *Corporate planning and performance management cycle (UK Clearing Bank)*

Quality Initiatives

Quality initiatives are important elements of improving service in many organisations. Performance management needs to integrate well with these initiatives; sometimes it may be introduced specifically as part of a quality initiative.

Kathleen Guin[1] argues 'that the process of performance management actually reinforces total quality management (TQM). Because it gives managers the skills and tools to carry out the "management" part of the TQM, performance management can enable managers to sustain TQM as a vital part of the organisation's culture. To be most effective, senior managers should model principles of performance management, give line management "ownership" and make sure performance management is integral to the way they do business.'

She states that a performance management process that reinforces TQM differs significantly from traditional performance appraisal in five ways:

1. Customer expectations, not job descriptions, generate the individual's performance expectations.
2. Results expectations meet different criteria than management-by-objectives statements.
3. Performance expectations include behavioural skills that make the real difference in achieving quality performance and total customer satisfaction.
4. The rating scale reflects actual performance, not a 'grading curve'.
5. Employees are active participants in the process, not merely 'drawn in' to management's actions.

In TQM environments the benchmarks for quality and customer service never remain static. The approach to performance management is one of constantly defining, achieving and redefining performance in a way that keeps every job challenging. A well-designed performance management should in itself be a 'quality' process – meeting or exceeding internal customer expectations, focusing employees on quality objectives and developing management processes and behaviours that build a motivating workplace climate.

A research and development department in a US chemical manufacturing company embarked on a TQM programme. It decided to incorporate total quality management into its performance appraisal process whose reputation within the company was not too favourable.

The department found that laboratory supervisors hated to prepare and deliver performance appraisals almost as much as their subordinates hated to receive and endure them. So the big issue for the department was to determine what kind of 'quality' performance review process could replace the existing and unsatisfactory one.

The department wanted to create an atmosphere where supervisors and subordinates worked in partnership to focus on the ultimate judge of performance: the customer. The new process was to take into account the views of the internal customers – the employees.

So what were the customer expectations? All employees were asked 'What are your expectations of how you should be managed?'

They gave some interesting answers:

- They wanted to be evaluated on their performance.
- They wanted feedback so that they could continually improve their jobs and grow in professional competence.
- They wanted some support from management.
- They expected to be recognised and rewarded for their achievements.
- Furthermore, they expected managers to foster a working atmosphere where the values of fairness, truth-telling, promise-keeping and respect for the individual were paramount.

This survey of employee attitudes made it clear that the traditional performance appraisal process was not meeting their expectations. It was regarded as being one-sided and focused more on boss-pleasing activity than on employee-satisfying activities. The bottom line was that the reviews were not effective at providing a quality product for either management or the employee.

The new performance management process was based on the premise that the employee (ie the customer) knows more or can learn better from anyone else, including the supervisor, about his or her capabilities, developmental needs and personal goals. That is why the responsibility for performance, personal development and achievement of full potential in the current job was given to the employee. The new process became employee-driven and intimately bonded to the total quality management process.

The TQM process is linked to the new process through the commitment that each individual will meet the agreed-upon expectations of internal and external customers all the time. The new process became the TQM response to the internal customer expectations. With the new process supervisors and staff work together to meet and exceed the customer's expectations. The employee is responsible for customer satisfaction, which forms the basis for the entire process. The supervisor acts as coach and mentor in achieving agreed-upon customer expectations and growth of the individual.

Selection Processes

When looking at an individual for promotion, performance management should provide valuable information on performance in current job and future potential, particularly if the review of performance focuses on the individual's competencies. Some organisations have an explicit link between the two processes.

Training and Development Processes

The more effective performance management processes integrate with training and development planning. Effective performance management is able to identify individual strengths and weaknesses which provide the basis for assessing individual development needs. Sometimes professional development reviews run alongside the performance management process.

Culture Change Programmes

Performance management processes have the power to change 'culture' (how things are done/how people behave/the values of the organisation). A well implemented performance management process can win the 'hearts and minds' of managers and other employees and can create a significant shift in managerial behaviours. This will help to change the culture of the organisation.

The three examples which follow show how different organisations have used the performance management process to change outmoded cultures.

Example 1 – A large UK Clearing Bank

Three thousand retail bank managers received a total of five days training in the key elements of performance management – planning, managing and reviewing. The managing phase focused on developing empowering/coaching management styles and the giving of regular constructive and honest feedback. These behaviours were not common in the company. Staff were used to being told what to do; they were not used to giving/receiving constructive feedback/praise; two-way dialogues on performance throughout the year were not common. The new performance management process changed these behaviours – but it took time. The bank audited the process annually and concluded that it would take three to four years before all managers 'got on board' with the new managerial behaviours.

Four years after the performance management process had been implemented the bank regarded the initiative as the 'biggest management development programme' it had ever initiated. It had made a major impact on the culture change programme.

Example 2 – A Public Health Education Authority

An organisation change programme had been drawn up to reinforce a new structure and work processes. The organisation set up three task forces to examine what changes needed to be made in three key HR areas in order to support the 'new' organisation – reward; performance management; defining work/roles (Figure 7.9).

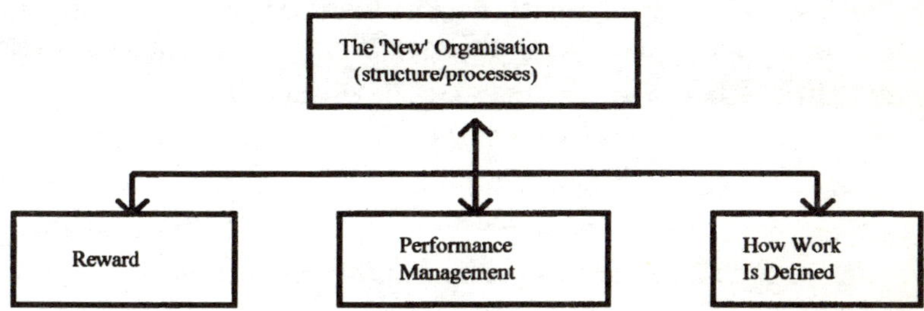

Figure 7.9 *The task force*

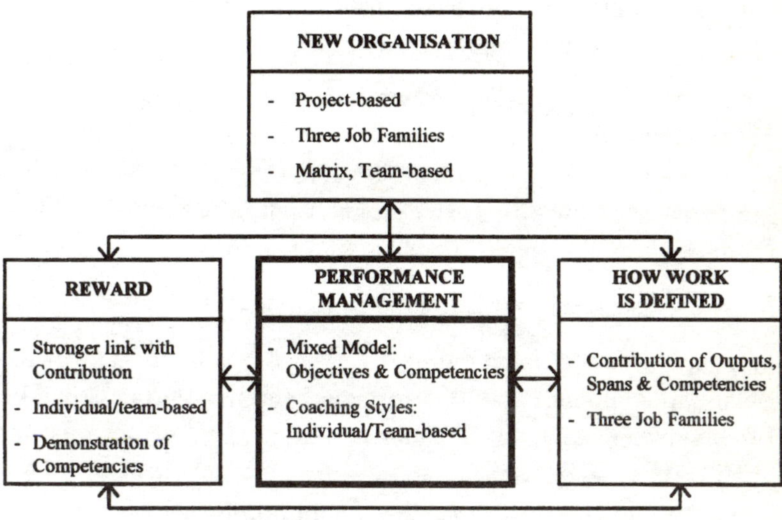

Figure 7.10 *The integrated HR process*

Each task force produced a set of proposals for changing the existing HR arrangements, and these were coordinated by a Central Steering Group. Figure 7.10 shows what the final integrated HR processes looked like.

Example 3 – A Chemical Manufacturing Company

This company used a new performance management process to deliver 'an Achievement Culture'. For many years it was a highly profitable company but during the late 1980s it began making substantial losses because of greater competition and, in particular, cheap imports flooding the European markets. The company had a clear choice – either to cease trading or to restructure and attempt to become profitable once more. It chose the latter course of action and after reducing the workforce by a substantial amount, embarked on a 'culture change' programme. The aim was to get the people remaining in the business much more focused in their activities and achieving better 'bottom-line' results. The concept of the 'Achievement Culture' was born. In a series of workshops, the employees of the company were asked what 'Achievement Culture' meant to them. Their responses were interesting:

- ❑ to know the 'big picture', ie what the company's objectives and priorities were;
- ❑ to have clearer individual/team objectives;
- ❑ to focus (and reward) on achievement not effort;
- ❑ to receive more support in achieving objectives.

They were asked what should be different:

- ❑ managers should listen more;
- ❑ two-way dialogues about performance throughout the year;
- ❑ freedom to make own decisions (and to accept responsibility for actions);
- ❑ constructive and regular feedback about performance;
- ❑ more sharing of objectives within and between teams to give a common sense of purpose;
- ❑ greater recognition for achievement.

The company's change programme focused on two main objectives. First, to get a smarter link between the business planning process and the setting of team/individual plans. Secondly, to develop those managerial behaviours which would reinforce the new culture. A new performance management process was designed to deliver these objectives.

At the heart of the new process was a performance management cycle which was split into four phases.

1. **Planning** – where individual objectives are linked to business targets.
2. **Managing** – where progress is reviewed and supportive managerial behaviours are demonstrated. The managerial behaviours such as providing clarity, listening, delegating, supporting and coaching were established as being at the heart of an Achievement Culture.
3. **Reviewing** – the formal annual review of actual performance against agreed objectives (both business-related and personal development objectives).
4. **Recognition** – linking the performance achieved (at company, team and individual levels) to the reward system.

The company defined a set of 'values' to reinforce the Achievement Culture. These were defined as:

- ❑ a commitment to safety and health;
- ❑ a commitment to customer satisfaction;
- ❑ a commitment to continuous improvement;
- ❑ better team working;
- ❑ a respect for individuals;
- ❑ a recognition of achievement.

All employees were involved in defining the behavioural indicators for each value. These indicators made it possible to assess the extent to which each value was being regularly demonstrated by line managers.

Also, the company audited the range of management styles used by individual managers throughout the business. Most managers tended to be 'pacesetters' and there was little use of a 'coaching' style (which the company wished to encourage). Each manager was able to compare his or her style profile against the one which the company was trying to encourage. Managers were given advice and counselling on how to change their styles.

By defining the behaviours and styles it expected, and by giving managers guidance on how to change their behaviours and styles and then auditing what changes were taking place, the company was able to focus all staff on the things that needed to change and was able to bring about real culture change. The performance management process was critical in bringing about a transformation over a period of two to three years. The company's business performance improved and most staff felt that managers were displaying more supportive behaviours throughout the performance management cycle.

SUMMARY

This chapter has illustrated the potential power of a performance management process which takes a holistic approach. Performance management should not be a 'stand alone' process. If it is integrated with other human resource processes it can add much more value to the organisation and becomes an essential element of an integrated approach to human resource management.

Reference

1. Guin, K A (1992) *Successfully Integrating Total Quality and Performance Appraisal* The Human Resources Professional, Spring, Faulkner and Gray, New York

Chapter 8

Total Performance Management

WHAT IS TOTAL PERFORMANCE MANAGEMENT?

The justifiable criticism of traditional performance appraisal schemes is that they are too often focused on a very narrow definition of what performance means in particular jobs. Usually a set of objectives/goals/targets are used to define the performance outputs for an individual job for a particular year. Sometimes the objectives are related to bigger corporate objectives, sometimes not. Occasionally they might cover aspects of the whole job; mostly not. So the traditional approach is a very one-dimensional output model of job performance (see Figure 8.1).

Total performance management is moving beyond this one-dimensional approach. In recent years many organisations have integrated competencies into the performance management process so that job expectations can be defined in terms of *what* results have to be achieved and *how* they are to be achieved. This is an input and output model, known as a 'mixed model' (Figure 8.2).

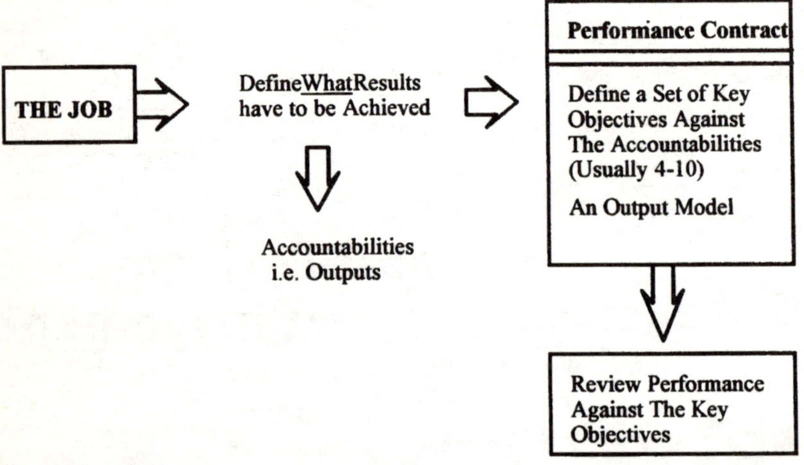

Figure 8.1 *'The one-dimensional model'*

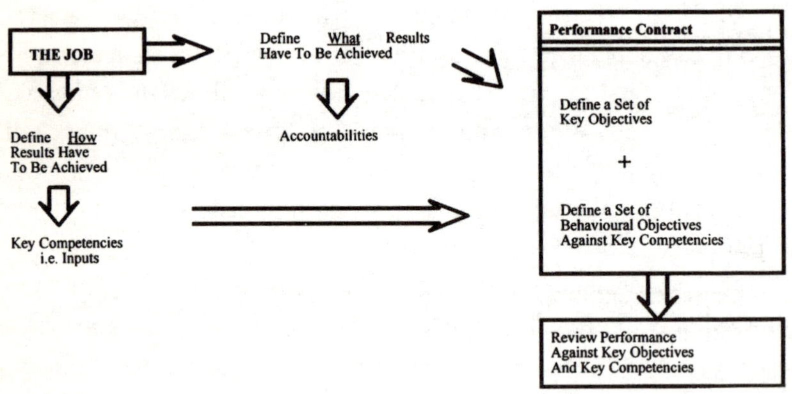

Figure 8.2 *'The mixed model'*

Total performance management can be extended to take account of a third dimension – the customer. The customer is involved in setting the performance contract and on giving feedback to the performance review. This is illustrated in Figure 8.3.

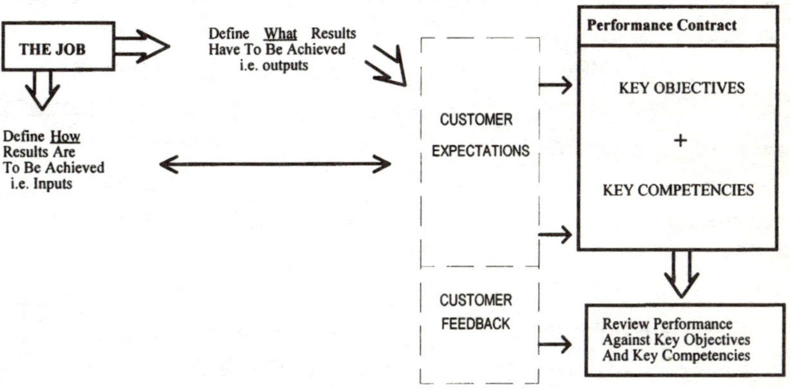

Figure 8.3 *'The 3 dimensional model'*

THE EMERGENCE OF MIXED MODELS

When I wrote a Performance Management Guide for Hay Consultants in 1991 there was a small section which described how competencies could fit into a performance management process. At that time I could find only one example of an organisation which had tried this approach. The typical performance management process of that time focused almost entirely on defining 'what' was to be achieved. However, today competency-based performance management schemes are plentiful and are becoming the model for the future. A performance management process that combines planning, managing and reviewing of both job results and competencies is called a 'mixed model'. These mixed models assess and reward both results and demonstration of competencies; both what employees actually deliver and how they do it. The mixed model represents a more powerful and longer-lasting approach to performance management than just an objectives-based approach. Fortunately, now there are many examples of good practice mixed models available.

A competency-based approach brings a different perspective to performance management. It uses a wider, more comprehensive language to describe the performance expected from an employee. Performance is defined in terms of the results and also in terms of the behaviours employees use to achieve the job results.

Figure 8.4 (which was devised by Spencer and Spencer[1]) shows how performance and competence are balanced in mixed models. In a line job achievement of job results might be weighted 90 per cent and demonstration of competencies only 10 per cent. At the other extreme, for example, in a customer service role, competence might be weighted 100 per cent.

Performance ('pay for results')	**Competencies ('pay for skill')**
❑ 'What' of performance. ❑ Quantitative measures. ❑ Short time frame (usually one year). ❑ Results oriented.	❑ 'How' of performance. ❑ More qualitative. ❑ Longer time frame (future performance). ❑ Development (behaviour change) oriented.

Figure 8.4 *The 'mixed' model approach*

In most mixed models, achievement of performance results is quantified, past oriented, and tied to department/unit objectives, based on the short term and used to make reward decisions. Competency-based review is more qualitative (although we will see examples of where competencies are 'measured' on a rating scale), longer term focused, future oriented and used for employee development and career path planning.

DEFINING COMPETENCIES

So what are competencies? The Hay/McBer definition describes a competency as 'a characteristic of an individual that has been shown to drive superior job performance'. Thus there is some causal link between certain behaviours and the achievement of superior job success. Competencies describe what makes people effective in a given role. This means that performance in most roles can be assessed by direct comparison of competencies demonstrated during a given review period with the competency requirements of the job.

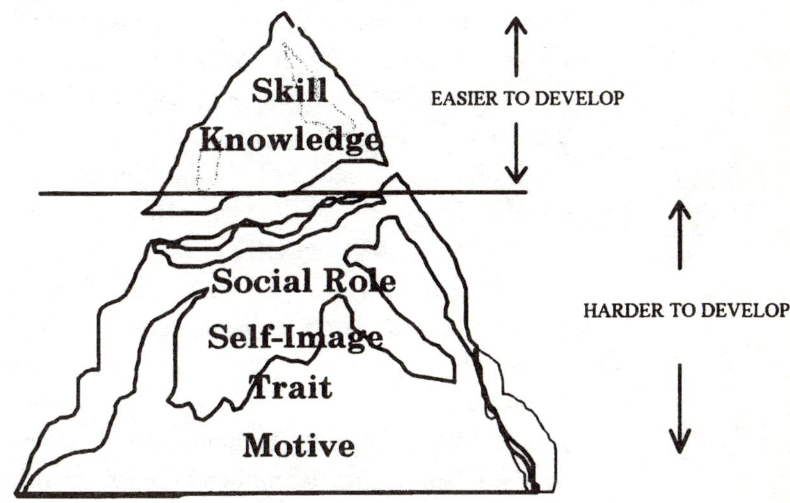

Figure 8.5 *The 'Iceberg' model of competencies*

Competencies can be enlikened to an iceberg, with knowledge and skills forming the top (ie above the water) and being clearly visible. The underlying elements of competencies are less visible. Social role and self-image exist at a conscious level; traits and motives exist further below the surface and are relevant to performance management only to the extent that they become observable.

What do these terms mean?

Skill:	Proficiency in an activity learned through repetition. Examples include typing, negotiating and supervising others.
Knowledge:	Visible information in a given area. Examples: knowing how to process documents with Word Perfect; knowing company policies and procedures for developing an annual department budget.
Social role:	A pattern of individual behaviours that is reinforced by membership of a social group or organisation – 'the outer self'. Examples: being either a leader or a follower, either initiating change or resisting it.
Self-image:	An individual's conception of their identity, personality and worth as a person – 'the inner self'. Examples: seeing oneself as a leader, seeing oneself as a motivator and developer of people. Self-image is an issue for performance management only when it is expressed as an observable behaviour.
Trait:	A relatively enduring characteristic of an individual's behaviour. Examples: being a good listener; having a sense of urgency. Traits become part of performance management only when they can be expressed as observable behaviours.
Motives:	Thoughts in a particular area – achievement, affiliation, or power – that drive, direct and select an individual's behaviour. Examples: wanting to achieve individually or wanting to influence the performance of others. Motives are also a part of performance management but only when they can be expressed as observable behaviours.

Why are competencies important?

The language of competencies provides a common framework and vocabulary for describing people, jobs and the systems that bring people into roles, develop them through the roles, reward them and pass them on to the next role. A competency is also a definition of role excellence – since it is based on the behaviours associated with superior performance. For the individual employee it means an understanding not only of the key objectives to be achieved but also of what behaviours are needed to achieve these objectives. Competency definitions provide a framework for understanding what kinds of behaviours can and should be used to satisfy key objectives most effectively.

Competency definitions are also important because they help employees recognise the kinds of behaviours which distinguish competent from superior performance. While skills and knowledge are necessary for top performance, they are not sufficient to guarantee it. The underlying competencies often suggest behaviours that lead to longer term success and ensure that key objectives are met.

Example

The importance of having a competency framework to describe the performance expectations in a job and to assess individual performance achievement is illustrated in the story of John, a computer systems designer in a Dutch software company.

John joined the company at the age of 25. He was regarded as a 'high-potential' graduate. From the start he was one of the best systems designers in the team. Figure 8.6 shows John's score on the company selection questionnaire in combination with the job demands.

This example shows that John fitted in very well with the job competency requirements. His know-how, ability to think in an analytical way and his strong competitive spirit (achievement orientation) made him very suitable. Although he lacked in a few other aspects, eg organisational awareness, it is no surprise that he was an excellent performer in his first job.

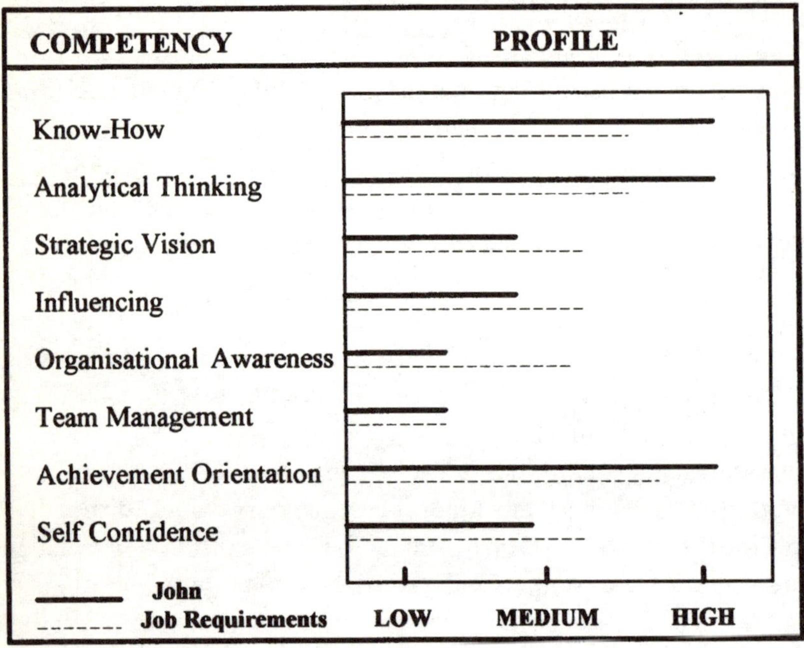

Figure 8.6 *John versus job requirements in first job*

His career proceeded excellently. He took on larger projects and handled them successfully. He was being stretched and he coped well. After a few successful years he was promoted to Technical Manager – a manager of managers.

In the early days in this role all seemed well, but after a time his performance lacked a certain acuteness of judgement. A significant number of important decisions were taken without consulting him. There were complaints that John should concentrate on the broad outlines of policy and not on the details of projects.

The important question is of course: how could this have happened? His start was very promising and he held several managerial posts with great success. Figure 8.7 shows John's profile in comparison with the job demands of his last job.

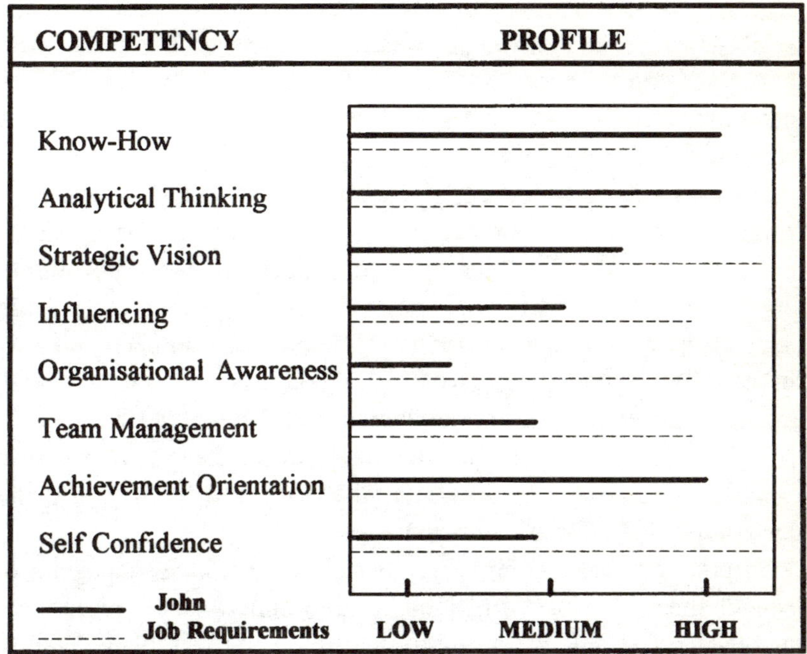

Figure 8.7 *John versus job requirements in his technical manager job*

In comparison with his previous job, his new role required a much greater independent development of vision, and the ability to 'take people with you', to gain their commitment to his vision – in other words strong team leadership qualities and the ability to recognise and persuade the key players in the organisation ('organisational awareness'). This job did not really challenge his expertise and mental acuteness. What he did, however, was to concentrate too much on the technical content of projects and too little on the business environment, both in a strategic and organisational sense. As a result of this behaviour his isolation increased and he could not exert any real influence. He preferred to do everything by himself. The essence of the problem was really that John was motivated to excel himself ('achievement orientation') instead of managing in such a way that others could excel.

So John's performance tailed off. He is still able to function reasonably well in the new job but there is a real possibility that he will feel increasingly uncomfortable and that his contribution towards the company will not be optimised. This is a clear case of insufficient use of talent.

The great advantage of a competency-based framework for a performance management process is that extra dimension it gives to the manager and job holder for setting performance expectations and for analysing performance gaps. In John's case, an early diagnosis of the match between John's demonstrated competencies and the new job competency requirements could have led to remedial actions aimed to create stronger visionary and team leadership qualities in John. An even earlier diagnosis would have revealed that John was unlikely to be a good fit to the new job without some prior development of certain competencies.

So properly used, competency-based performance management is much more likely to bring about long-term performance improvement. The competency job profile provides a template against which individual job holders can be compared and a model of what 'superior performers' do.

However, it has to be said that even obtaining a perfect match of job/job holder competencies does not guarantee superior performance. We know that someone's ultimate job performance is the combined result of the types of competency he/she has matched against job requirements and the situation in which they are working. How people are managed and the 'climate' of the workplace are critical factors in influencing how individuals perform. This issue is discussed in Chapter 10.

Where is a competency-based approach appropriate?

Competency-based performance management processes are becoming more prevalent in many organisations, but they are particularly appropriate for organisations where there are:

- *Uncertain environments:* in certain and rapidly changing environments, where results are not under employee control, hard results objectives are often rendered irrelevant by external events, eg in banking organisations where changes in commercial base rates affect mortgage and commercial lending targets. In such situations, assessment of performance must be based on whether employees did everything they could, whether they demonstrated the right behaviours which would in other circumstances have led to successful achievements. The less control employees have over results, the more performance should be based on demonstration of competencies.

- *Qualitative/process service jobs:* in jobs with no relevant measurable outcomes – qualitative skills – competencies – are the best indication of employee performance, eg for general assistants in supermarket chains – competency behaviours – such as being friendly and helpful to irritable customers, being well organised and tidy minded, anticipating customer enquiries – are the job requirements. The more subjective the job output, the more important it is to use competency definitions as the basis for the performance management process.
- *Self-managed teams:* in teams, individual results outputs may be less important than contribution to the group process. Team work/leadership competencies are increasingly important in organisations. The more important team performance is, as opposed to individual performance, the more important it is to appraise the teamwork and cooperation behaviours of individual employees.
- *'Developmental' jobs:* where particular jobs are designed to 'grow'. The more a job stresses the development of skills, eg management trainee positions, the more appraisal should be based upon demonstration of competencies.
- *Changing organisations:* in changing environments, employees' potential to contribute to the organisation in the future may be more important than their past performance. Most performance management systems are past oriented. The greater the emphasis on future performance, the more the performance management process should use the competency framework to stress the development and appraisal of competencies.

STEPS IN DEVELOPING A COMPETENCY-BASED PERFORMANCE MANAGEMENT PROCESS

There are three key steps:

1. Identify the competencies required for superior performance in present or future jobs. To add value, a performance management process should motivate employees to do better than their current actual performance.
2. Develop a 'mixed model' performance management process for defining and assessing both job results and competency behaviours that predict performance in the job.
3. Train all staff in performance management (eg coaching for performance improvement).

Let us look at examples of how two companies integrated a competency-based approach into existing performance management processes. The first case is a large international company which, for this purpose of this case study, we shall call 'Euroservice'.

Case 1: Euroservice

In the early 80s Euroservice started a programme aimed at attaching much more importance to the performance of the individual worker. Under the name of 'Performance '80' an extensive programme was started to extend the already existing management by objectives for business unit managers to the total population of workers. Targets were formulated for all workers, which were derived from business plans and job accountabilities. The remuneration system was linked to achieving these individual targets. These were the results:

- ❑ the performance of the workers hardly improved;
- ❑ an unhealthy competition between workers obstructed team work;
- ❑ it was difficult to motivate people to make innovative contributions because these were regarded as inherently risky.

Euroservice was surprised that the performance had not improved. They had foreseen potential difficulties with individual competition and risk-avoiding behaviour, and had hoped to avoid them through senior managers taking corrective action. At this stage, they did not see many opportunities to stimulate individual performance.

During the analysis of the disappointing results it emerged that the predominant cause was that managers had no idea *how* to direct performance. If a worker was in danger of not reaching his target, the manager could point this out to him. In the most favourable case he could offer him ideas on how to reach the agreed-upon target. However, he could do that *before* the introduction of 'Performance '80', so in that sense not very much had changed. In addition the managers were also aware of their task to stimulate team development and innovative behaviour. However, they did not know how to do this.

Euroservice was confronted with the essence of leadership: 'managers determine the difference'. In order to enable managers to give practical meaning to this, three objectives were undertaken:

1. besides individual performance targets, team targets were also identified;
2. competency profiles were drawn up;
3. in training, the managers were made aware of the relation between their own actions on the performance of their teams.

Individual and team targets

The company wished to hold on to concrete output as the primary focus in the work. Although 'Performance '80' was not a success, a clear output orientation had been developed which the company wished to retain. Subsequently, however, the variable income of the workers was no longer made dependent on achieving individual targets. When establishing the variable incomes, a mixture of company targets, team targets and individual targets was used. This mixture varied for each category of jobs and was formulated again each year during the budgeting rounds.

Competency profiles

One of the greatest objections to the above-mentioned system was that managers could only assess individual targets according to output criteria. They only assessed *what* they expected of persons and not *how* these persons could achieve these results. The latter is absolutely necessary to actually assist workers and as a result to direct their performance.

In order to solve this problem, jobs were clustered. In the whole organisation 20 job clusters were identified, for example: senior general management, middle general management, managers of professional groups, senior staff members, junior staff members and sales persons. For these twenty groups competency profiles were compiled. It was established which type of behaviours of job practitioners in these clusters led to success. With this information the managers could improve their staff performance considerably.

Instead of telling sales person X about a backlog in the realisation of his sales budget, the sales manager could, for example, together with the employee, see whether he had shown the influencing behaviour which, when drawing up the competency profile, had led the best sales persons to their successes.

Training of managers

One of the most important environmental factors determining the behaviour of persons in the end is the work climate. If one's own freedom and responsibility are low, if the standards for performance are low, if workers are punished more than rewarded, if there is little pride and involvement, persons with the 'right' competency profile may still underperform. The question is always: as a manager, how does one achieve a motivating environment which brings out the best in people? To answer this question, and also to be able to do something about it, all the executive staff of Euroservice were put through Hay's Excelling Manager programme. In this programme all managers were assessed in respect to three factors:

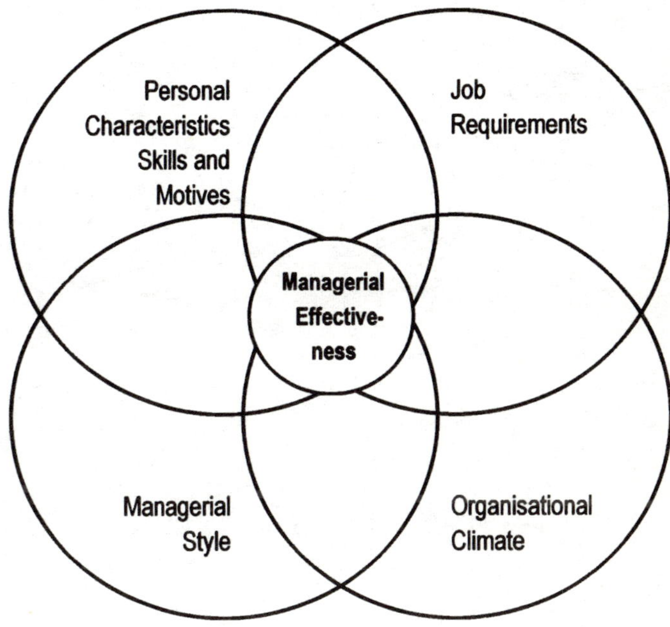

Figure 8.8 *Four key factors affecting organisational performance*

1. Their own individual competency profile versus that of their job.
2. Their management styles.
3. The work climate in their work unit.

The relationship between these factors is shown in Figure 8.8.

Our second example is taken from a world renowned fertiliser manufacturing company which redesigned its performance management process, to make it an instrument of culture change. We shall call this company 'Z Fertiliser Ltd'.

Case 2: Z Fertiliser Ltd

During the 1980s this company's fortunes dropped dramatically. The once very profitable business was hit by a flood of cheap imports into the European market. In 1991 the company restructured and determined to turn the business around. It decided that it needed to change managerial behaviours. A competency profile for senior managers was drawn up and integrated into the performance management process. The new competencies were:

- ❑ Team leadership
- ❑ Achievement orientation
- ❑ Customer focus
- ❑ Concern for quality
- ❑ Developing others
- ❑ Direct influencing.

These competencies were used in the review phase of the performance management process. For each competency a set of behavioural indicators was drawn up against which each manager could assess themselves or be assessed by others.

Direct influencing

Direct influencing is the ability to develop and use effective strategies to influence others. Strategies involve sequences of actions or alternatives that are calculated in advance and which incorporate aspects of two other competencies (persuasiveness and concern with personal impact).
Appraisal: How often does the job holder demonstrate the behaviour in an effective way, when opportunities are given?

4 Very frequently
3 In some situations
2 Not very often
1 Never

Selects and screens information to others	4	3	2	1
Uses subtle strategies to influence others	4	3	2	1
Uses experts or third parties to influence others	4	3	2	1
Makes others feel ownership of one's own proposal	4	3	2	1
Overall rating	**4**	**3**	**2**	**1**

With the introduction of these competencies, each manager was required to draw up a new style performance plan with his line manager. This plan consisted of two elements: job objectives and personal development objectives (see Figure 8.9).

PERFORMANCE PLAN	
Job Objectives	**Development Objectives**
e.g. Sell X tons of firtiliser A at £y per ton.	e.g. Take District Manager on sales vistits (use of third parties to influence others – influencing strategies).

Figure 8.9 *The new style performance plan*

This mixed model focused managers on the results they have to achieve and thc behaviours they have to demonstrate in achieving them. There is no doubt that this process helped to clarify what behaviours were expected and over the course of 2–3 years there has been a significant shift in the workplace climate and in the fortunes of the company.

SOME COMPETENCY PROFILES

On pages 121 and 122 there are a number of competency profiles for different jobs:

Sales Manager

Competencies
Focus on client needs
Building partnership with client
Interpersonal sensitivity
Achievement orientation
Concern for quality
Organisational awareness
Team leadership

eg Organisational awareness
Definition: An accurate understanding of others at the organisational level – their feelings, their reasons for their actions and interaction, their intentions. It also involved understanding how organisations function and how people function in organisations.

Behavioural indicators (examples):

1. Response to explicit customer requests only.
2. Recognises formal customer hierarchy.
3. Recognises organisational constraints, understands informal interactions within customer organisations.
4. Understands key decision makers and the power and politics of the organisation.

Senior Manager

Competencies
Analytical thinking
Pattern recognition
Strategic thinking
Persuasion
Use of influence strategies
Personal impact
Motivating

eg Pattern recognition
Definition: The ability to identify patterns or connections between situations that are not obviously related and to identify the key or underlying issues in complex situations.

Behavioural indicators (examples):

1. Sees connections or patterns not obvious to others.
2. Condenses large amounts of data to useful form.
3. Uses clear analogies in speech and writing.
4. Rapidly identifies key issues in a complex situation.

Clerical Assistant

Competencies
Concern for quality
Team work
Interpersonal understanding
Achievement orientation
Communication
Information seeking
Expertise

eg Information seeking
Definition: An underlying curiosity, a desire to know about more things, people or issues; making an effort to get more information, not accepting situations at face value.

Behavioural indicators (examples):
1. Collects the facts needed to make arrangements and answers basic queries.
2. Asks questions for clarification and checks accuracy.
3. Makes telephone enquiries to find out basic information.
4. Cross-checks information before circulating it or acting on it.

Chief Inspector of Police

Competencies
Communication skills
Interpersonal skills
Problem solving
Decision making
Creativity
Resilience
Achievement orientation

eg Communication skills
Definition: Able to speak and write in ways that get the message across; and to translate one's own thoughts or those of others into meaning.

Behavioural indicators (examples):
1. Listens carefully to people who want information and analyses what they want.
2. Communicates real and anticipated problems and proposed solutions effectively.
3. Communicates incisively what individual/team tasks are about.
4. Effectively communicates major issues and policies to the media.

Competency-based performance management shifts the emphasis of appraisal from just the job results achieved to the behaviours and competencies demonstrated in achieving those results. Diagnosis and problem solving to deal with poor performance takes this form:

> If results are not at the desired level, give higher priority to these job objectives, demonstrate these behaviours more often, and develop these competencies.

The addition of competencies to the performance management process has important implications for how people are managed. Managers have to commit themselves to providing employees with coaching and other competency development activities during the performance cycle.

Therefore the most important factor in implementing a competency-based performance management process is the training of managers to provide this coaching and developmental assistance. This issue is explored in later chapters.

AN EXAMPLE OF A 'TOTAL PERFORMANCE MANAGEMENT' PROCESS

So far there are relatively few examples of organisations which have taken the full Total Performance Management route, ie added the third dimension – the customer – to the performance management process.

In one example from the United States – a large chemical manufacturing company – its 'Performance Excellence' process was based on 4 key principles:

1. Customer focus
2. Management support
3. Total employee involvement
4. Continuous improvement.

Customer input is regarded as an important feedback tool for helping employees to continuously improve their performance and for helping to assess employees' performance objectively. The company uses a customer feedback worksheet (Figure 8.10) to gather views from internal and external customers during the performance planning phase. Also it uses a customer feedback form to gather data for the performance review phase (Figure 8.11).

Internal customers

Customer Name	Customer's Expectations/ Requirements	On-going	Completion Date

External customers

Customer Name	Customer's Expectations/ Requirements	On-going	Completion Date

Figure 8.10: *Customer Feedback Worksheet*

<table>
<tr><td colspan="2">To help us achieve our goals of continuous performance improvement and development of each employee and customer focus, please let me know how well ______________ is meeting your agreed-upon expectations and requirements.</td></tr>
<tr><td>EXPECTATIONS/REQUIREMENTS</td><td>RESULTS</td></tr>
<tr><td>❑
❑
❑
❑</td><td>❑
❑
❑
❑</td></tr>
<tr><td colspan="2">Major strengths:</td></tr>
</table>

Figure 8.11 *Customer feedback form*

During the performance planning discussion, the manager and employee identify the employee's key internal or external customers and complete the customer feedback worksheet. They agree that the manager will get input from the customer at the end of the year or when the employee completes an important project or piece of work for the customer.

During informal coaching discussions through the year, the manager and employee revise the customer feedback worksheet as needed.

Before the performance review at the end of the year, the manager contacts the customer for feedback on the employee's performance, or uses information the manager gathered upon the employee's completion of a major project. The manager uses this feedback as one important factor in assessing the employee's performance. The manager may gather information from the customer face-to-face, by telephone or by asking the customer to complete the customer feedback form.

In our second example – an international human resource consultancy – client relationship management has been identified as a key competency for all consultants. Superior consultants are expected to be strongly oriented towards service to the client, including a sophisticated in-depth understanding of the individual client contacts, client organisation and their needs and the flexible use of influence strategies in relation to the client. Superior consultants should establish a longer term closer relationship with clients, ultimately leading to more business. The behavioural indicators which are used to assess the quality of client relationship management are:

- ❑ clear comprehensive client plans;
- ❑ evidence of understanding of client needs/issues;
- ❑ evidence of good relationships – visits and file notes;
- ❑ development of additional points of entry;
- ❑ evidence of active marketing to clients;
- ❑ up-to-date client contact lists;
- ❑ no complaints.

The company has established regular client satisfaction surveys to provide direct feedback from clients about the extent the company is meeting client expectations/requirements.

SUMMARY

The integration of competencies into the performance management process is a very significant development. It allows organisations to define 'total' performance both in terms of the short-term objectives required and the long-term development required in each job holder. By giving each job holder a picture of the competencies required for superior performance, the organisation is producing a very powerful process for self improvement. What it has to ensure is that managers and job holders understand what the competencies are and how they should be used in the performance management process.

Reference

1. Spencer, L and Spencer, S (1993) *Competence at Work,* Wiley, USA

Chapter 9

Fit With Work Cultures

ORGANISATIONAL CULTURE

In Chapter 3 we described how more organisations are developing flatter, more flexible structures in which empowered and multi-skilled work groups are increasingly important. However, despite this general development, the actual work environments within organisations will continue to differ. All of us have experienced cultural differences in organisations, that is, the way things are done; the likes and dislikes in behaviours, dress attitudes, leadership styles and communication.

Organisational culture is difficult to define. It is best described as a feeling which a number of people share consistently about work situations in the organisation: 'What it's like to work here'; 'the way we do things around here'. Professor Charles Handy[1] suggests that cultures are deeper phenomena than just commonly agreed ways of perceiving a situation:

> In organisations, there are deep set beliefs about the way work should be organised, the way authority should be exercised, people rewarded, people controlled. What are the

> degrees of formalisation required? How much planning, and how far ahead? What combination of initiative and obedience is looked for in subordinates? Are there rules and procedures or only results? These are all parts of the culture of an organisation.

Culture refers to the way people in different (or sometimes similar) work organisations view the world, their life, and the way they go about their work. Culture will differ within any one organisation too; different points of view might exist between those working in, for example, production, support services, sales and policy making.

Fitting the performance management process to the work culture

We have moved a long way from the notion that the performance management process comes in 'one size only' which is applied in the same way to any organisation, regardless of its shape, size, stage of development or culture. The proposition set out in this chapter is quite simple: all human resource management processes – like selection, performance management, management development, training and reward – should be aligned to the work cultures within the organisation.

A framework for defining work cultures

Hay Management Consultants have developed a framework for defining work cultures. Work culture is not something that happens by chance or at the whim or decree of the chief executive. Research by Hay indicates that work culture arises as a direct result of the strategic pressures which are driving the business, and the balance between these pressures. Four such pressures are key in determining work culture. These are shown in Figure 9.1.

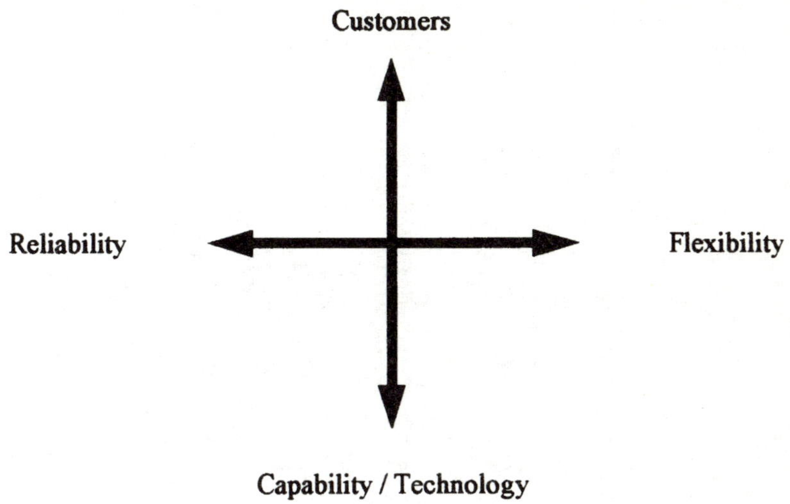

Figure 9.1 *The four strategic pressures which determine work culture*

Of course you are likely to say that all four pressures are critical to the success of your business. But it is useful to stand back and identify the primary drivers for your business – what are the predominant pulls? Where are the emphases? The balance between their results in the four work cultures is set out in Figure 9.2.

Few organisations will fit any one of these models exactly; many organisations will show different characteristics in different business units or operations.

THE FUNCTIONAL WORK CULTURE

If you conclude that the predominant pulls are about the reliable delivery of your internal capability or technology, then you are describing a *functional work culture*.

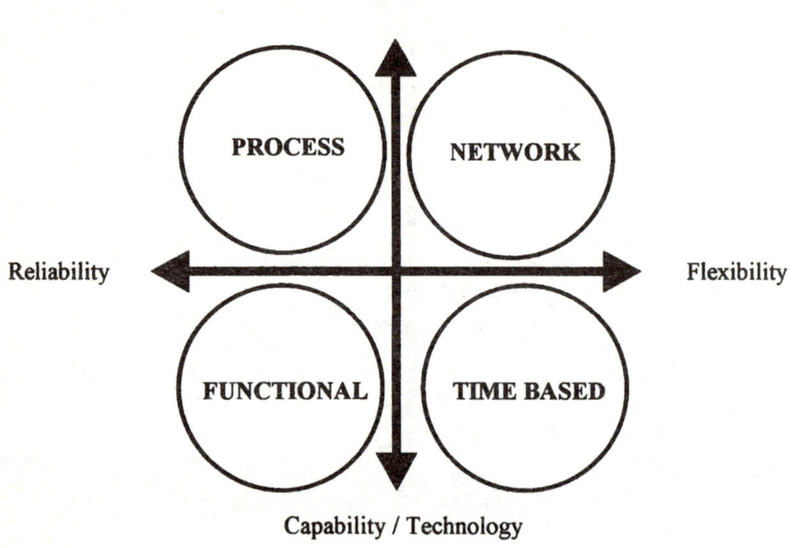

Figure 9.2 *Work culture models (Hay)*

Characteristics

Until the last decade or so, most companies were organised along 'functional' lines. Deep management hierarchies – with an emphasis on limited risk, internal order and job security – characterised these organisations, the emphasis being on technology, reliability and functional excellence. What is important is to have something you can do well, over and over again. You are likely to take limited risks, to specialise by function. Power resides in expertise, and in clearly defined control. Today, though many companies are moving away from this model, it remains a very effective structure for companies where high degrees of reliability are critical or for specialised units – the accounting functions, for instance – and in many areas of national and local government.

The functional organisation is going to get its competitive advantage from finding and applying core specialised knowledge and technology. This may be hard technology (like being the best in its application of material science) or softer know-how (like being the best at branding). This type of culture manages to ensure reliability, has strong management systems to exploit its know-how and tends to value hierarchy. It is a culture typical of some leading aerospace companies, as well as food companies.

Key Competencies

In the functional culture our research shows that with the heavy emphasis on technical competence, influence will tend to be rational and direct persuasion helps people to do this best. Thinking will tend to be very rational and analytical and because the timescales for programmes are usually longer, then tenacity will help people adapt to this environment. Because competitive advantage does come explicitly through defined skills, it will be a distinguishing feature, as will be the ability to develop others. There will be other competencies but these will be the ones which underpin the organisation.

How work is organised and rewarded

Work is likely to be organised into fairly well defined jobs and accountabilities with clear relationships between them. Almost certainly most organisations will have stripped out layers of hierarchy. Perhaps they will also be encouraging more flexibility, better collaboration between functions, and pushing responsibility down the line. But these do not change the fundamental relevance of the structure, and of clarity.

In functional work cultures, because jobs/roles are central to the way work is organised, they are likely to be central to pay. So job evaluation and grading are likely to be important components, moderated by the effects of performance and competence. Any element of team-based pay in this culture is likely to be at the macro-team level – in other words, company and unit-wide profit share or bonus.

The performance management process

In this work culture the effective performance management process will be based on the key outputs of individual jobs. But it could embrace those competencies which contribute to the successful achievement of key objectives. Individual job objectives should link with business plan objectives and there should be a formalised, planned process of tracking these objectives throughout the year (see Figure 9.3).

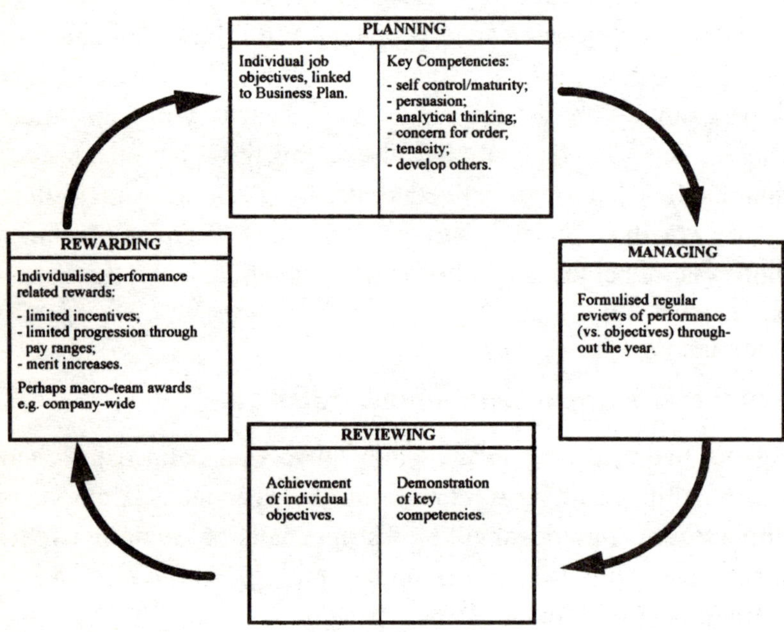

Figure 9.3. *The performance management process in a functional work culture*

Over the last few years there has been the risk of seeing the Functional Work Culture model as 'the old', and other models as 'the new' - with the obvious implication that old is bad, new is good. This is erroneous. It is quite clear that the functional work model will remain a valid model for many organisations or parts of organisations, and that applying newer, more fashionable approaches – highly relevant to other work cultures – may be ineffective, or worse, actually harmful.

But let us examine how many organisations are moving away from this work culture.

THE PROCESS WORK CULTURE

For many, the shift is towards customer orientation, while keeping reliability as a major requirement. This combination we call the *process work culture*. (See Figure 9.2).

Think about what is happening in many financial services companies, for example. Traditional structures are being replaced with multi-functional teams. Issues of process are taking over from issues of structure. Business process re-engineering is rife. Internal power is less embedded in established hierarchies, but instead lies in the concentration of mutual interest. Effectiveness is measured 'through the eyes of the customer'.

The process work culture organisation gets its competitive advantage by organising its total stream of business around delivery to the customer or markets. It is opposed to functional divisions if this prevents it from applying its assets to benefit the customer. Processes, including performance management, involve the customer directly.

Key Competencies

The use of influence has to be more subtle and better throughout than just direct, rational persuasion. To make the system work you need people using frameworks and larger concepts so you have to move to a different type of thinking than merely logical analysis. These are complex organisations that have to endure, so a fair amount of tenacity is still needed to adapt. Because they are driven by responding to customer needs, increasing levels of customer sensitivity are necessary in order to succeed. There will be a need for a higher level of team management competencies than in the functional cultures.

How work is organised and rewarded

The flexibility and teamwork required take some of the emphasis off traditional notions of the job, and put more stress on the contribution, skills and competencies of individuals.

In this work culture, the three pay factors (of role, performance and competence) are much more in balance. Roles are likely to be seen as levels of work in families, rather than jobs in structures, and expressed in terms of skills, competencies and outputs.

Table 9.1 is an example of an operations (project) family in a health education organisation.

Table 9.1 *An operations family in a health education organisation*

Levels	Outputs	Skills	Competencies
1/2	Washes up Cleans and tidies Sorts mail Retrieves data from storage Operates switchboard Takes messages	Knows routines Knows where things are Knows who is who Can operate simple machines	Tenacity 1 Concern for quality 1 Flexibility 1 Organisational commitment 1 Communications 1
10	Manages large significant projects Fosters good team climate in large teams Plans, monitors and controls use of substantial project resources	People management Being able to make things happen Monitoring team performance Project planning	Concern for quality 4 Team work 4 Communication 5 Initiative 3 Flexibility 3 Organisational commitment 3 Planning and organising 4 Information seeking 4

Individual pay will reflect this balance, with the links to skills, competencies and performance being much stronger and more explicit than in functional work cultures. Because of the focus on fairly stable teams, an element of team-based pay is likely to be relevant, generating bonus based on team performance.

The performance management process

To illustrate what an effective performance management process looks like in a process work culture let me quote from the personnel manager of a major UK insurance company which was transformed into a delayered, team-based organisation:

> Having designed the organisational structure and specified the roles, responsibilities and competencies, we then moved on to look at the pay and performance management processes. Clearly we had to have a performance management process that really reinforced the new culture. One of empowerment, openness and honesty; where continuous improvement would become a way of working. We introduced quarterly appraisals. Whilst the appraisals are conducted by the immediate manager, we have encouraged what we call 360° appraisal by getting formal input from subordinates and peers as well. A critical factor in ensuring that the feedback was objective was to put in place a whole series of information sources. Specifically we have set up a skills accreditation process for the assessment of technical skills of our case managers; we have management information systems which measure the productivity and turnaround times of individual case managers and the teams. We have competency questionnaires to assess individual competencies. Finally, we have fine-tuned all the cost and budget information. Ultimately, this process is linked to the pay review. When it comes to the annual pay review key performance indicators for all roles have been defined.
>
> In all cases the demonstration of competencies is an important pay factor as are measurable outputs from individuals and teams. This is supported by the setting of measurable objectives for each member of the management team.
>
> The final piece of the jigsaw in terms of pay is a team bonus. The objective of the bonus is to reinforce the teamworking aspect and particularly focus attention on the deliv-

ery of excellent customer service and the achievement of a reduction in costs.

	Case manager	Team leader	Customer service manager
Skills acquisition	✓		
Competencies	✓	✓	✓
Output (Timeliness, quality & productivity)	Individual and team	Case manager and team	Whole team
Personal objectives		✓	✓
Cost management			✓

TIME-BASED WORK CULTURE

The third kind of work culture emphasises technology and flexibility. Again it does not ignore the customer or reliability, but it does say: reduce the cycle time; make better use of the assets; exploit the technology; move ahead of the market; dominate and change the market; get there first. We call it the *time-based work culture.* (See Figure 9.2).

Characteristics

This model has been used by companies to assert market dominance and maximise return on assets. Organisations employing this model stress initiative and flexibility, flat structures, programme teams and multi-functional expertise. These types of organisations seek to dominate their markets during their highly profitable phase and then use the accumulated internal competencies of their people to move on to new or emerging market opportunities.

These organisations emphasise flexibility and agility. Think about computer manufacturers, fast-changing consumer goods, or about product development and internal change teams within organisations.

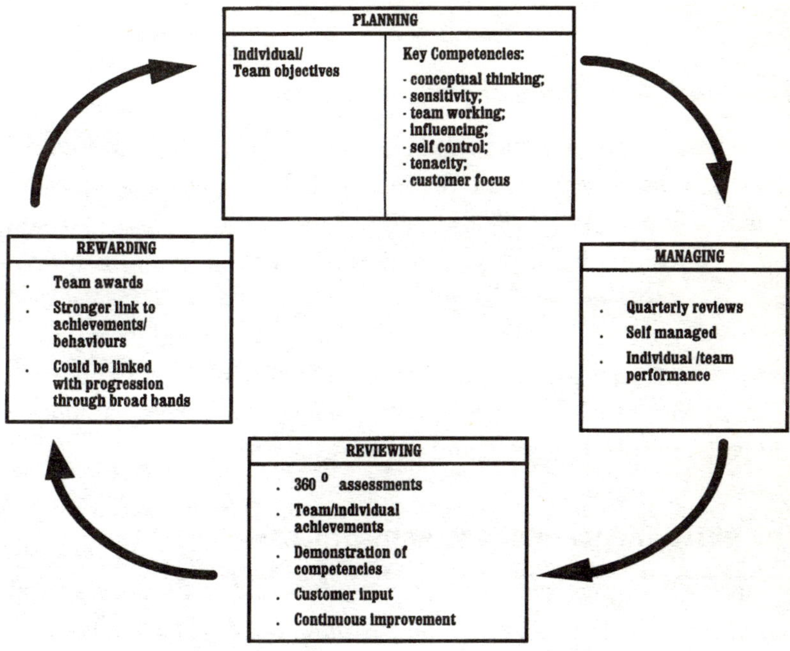

Figure 9.4 *The performance management process in a process work culture*

Key competencies

Because the culture is built around agility, then flexibility will tend to be much more critical to adapt to the organisation's needs. While this organisation does emphasise teamwork it emphasises much more the ability of individuals to have an impact, since responsiveness is the most critical factor of the organisation. When you put together a project team, you do not pick anonymous boxes on charts. You pick him or her. You pick a good engineer, your best marketeer, someone with organising capability, and so on. Therefore this type of organisation influences people through direct personal impact. The way that work gets done has to be against some precise time limits, therefore the ability to direct others effectively is important and initiative and self-confidence are greatly prized.

How work is organised and rewarded

Power resides not in structure, but in the particular mix of individual capability at any point in time, and in opportunity spotting. Formal structures are very flat and non-hierarchical. Real working relationships are about project teams which form and reform over time.

And so the balance in pay is more about people and their performance than about jobs or fixed roles. Individual pay is likely to be closely geared to demonstrated competence and delivery. Team pay will reflect project success and delivery.

The performance management process

In this work culture team members collaborate to produce a product/project which meets all of the customer needs. The team may be self-governed or managed by someone else in the organisation, eg executive sponsor. Equal contribution of team members is essential to meeting team goals. Communication is frequent and often formal in order to check progress against milestones and ensure the project is completed within tight deadlines (see Figure 9.5).

NETWORK WORK CULTURE

Finally, the fourth work culture is where the emphasis is on customers and flexibility. It involves individuals with specific – often unique – capabilities, coming together in a team which may subsequently break up and never work together again. This is the *network work culture.* (See Figure 9.2).

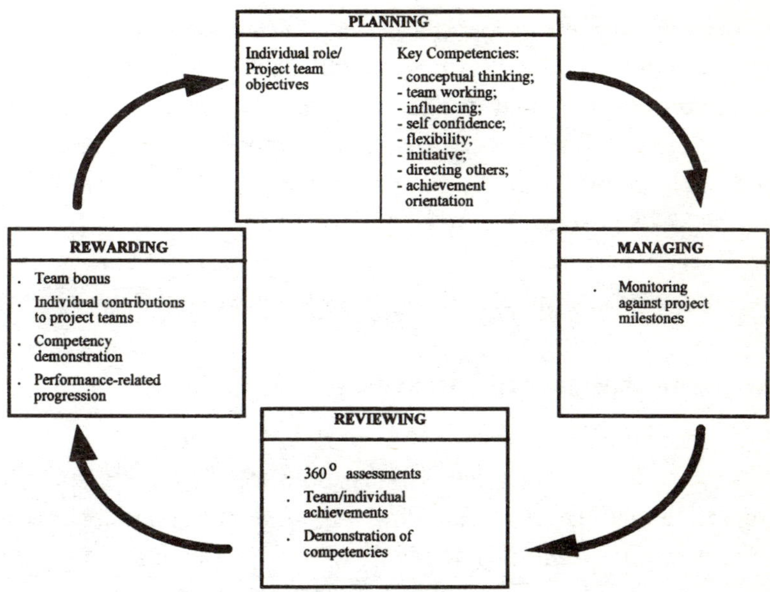

Figure 9.5 *The performance management process in a time-based work culture*

Characteristics

Here, *ad hoc* groups and temporary alliances create an organisation that ceases to exist after its goal is achieved. These organisations are innovative and flexible, creating value by bringing together key resources that can have an immediate impact on the market. People in this culture must be both pragmatic and trailblazing, with power residing with those who possess required critical skills and the ability to create strategic alliances.

These organisations exist to adapt to constant change. Entertainment companies, consultancies and construction companies are good examples of this type of culture.

Key competencies

The network culture influences largely through building relationships and more elaborate influence strategies since a key feature of this organisation is that it does not have control over all the resources. Flexibility will be particularly important as a characteristic to help people to adapt, but in the core of the organisation the thinking skills also need to be adaptable. Therefore the competency known as 'pattern recognition', which involves being able to produce concepts from unrelated data, will be most important.

How work is organised and rewarded

This work culture has very flexible work arrangements. Everything is geared around getting the 'best' people together for a specific purpose, eg making a firm, building a road, then disbanding. Pay is very much a question of individual contracts reflecting reputation, personal contribution. Base salary, as such, may be a low proportion of the total reward, or even non-existent.

The performance management process

This will be a highly individual, informal, contract-based process. There will be a high degree of self management. In some cases work will be carried out on a contract basis, with contractors typically paid on a *per diem* or contract basis, with fixed performance-related penalties and rewards. Contributions are required from all team members in order for the venture to be a success. Communication is situational and informal. The team leader must provide clear direction given the changes that can often occur in team membership. Figure 9.6 illustrates how a network work culture functions.

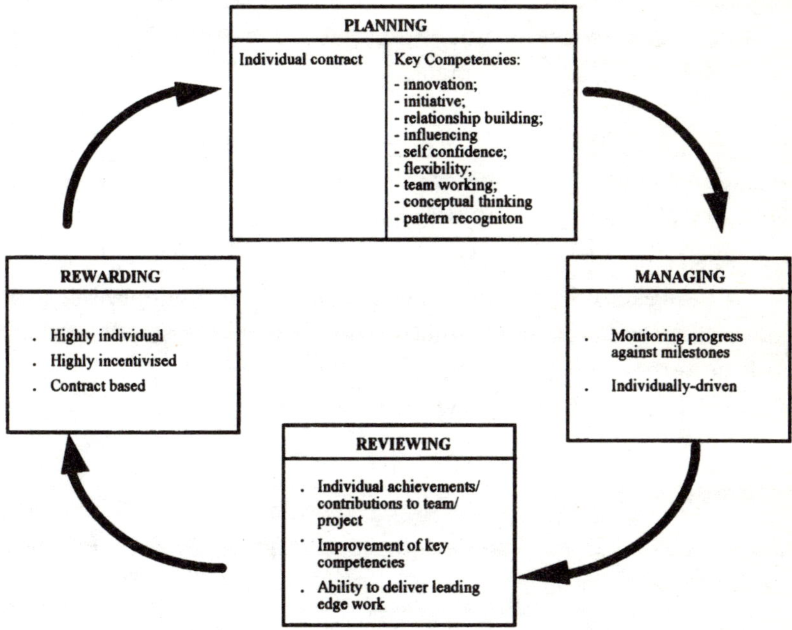

Figure 9.6 *The performance management process in a network work culture*

SUMMARY

This framework should help you to think through the most appropriate performance management and performance-related pay arrangements for your organisation. The key word is *appropriate*. There is no universal model which fits all organisations/work cultures. Team-based arrangements may be the ideal approach in some circumstances, and not in others. Competency-linked pay may really help in some work cultures, but be quite out of line for others. You have to tailor the arrangements which are dynamic and appropriate to your needs. And in doing so, recognise that it is not always possible, or appropriate, to categorise the whole organisation in terms of a single work culture. You might, for example, conclude that sales and manufacturing fit the functional model, long-term research might be more process oriented, while product development shows time-based characteristics.

It is likely that over the next few years we will see increasing diversity of performance management arrangements, not just between organisations, but also within organisations. Obviously this will have to be balanced by the need for some degree of corporate consistency. Such arrangements may not be the tidy, 'one size fits all' approach of traditional performance management, but they will be a much better fit to your organisation's strategy, values and work cultures. Because of this, they are more likely to be more effective and 'comfortable' within the organisation.

Reference

1. Handy, C (1976) *Understanding Organisations* Penguin Education, London

Chapter 10

A Motivating Work Climate

MANAGERIAL BEHAVIOURS MAKE A DIFFERENCE

In the previous chapter it was stressed that even if an employee has the competencies associated with superior performers it does not guarantee that the employee will produce successful performance. His or her actual performance is a product of the interaction of their competencies and the situation in which they are working. Many people have experienced the situation in their work when a line manager rules over his staff by taking decisions about the work to be carried out and the manner in which work is to be carried out. Perhaps they could have made valuable contributions, but the behaviour and attitudes of the manager blocked something in their own behaviour. Due to this, the manager felt justified to continue his own individualistic behaviour. 'Nobody has any ideas here, so I have to have them.' A talented person may dry up completely when working for such a manager.

We know from our research we have done over many years that about 30 per cent of the variance in individuals' discretionary efforts is attributed to the climate in which they work. The atmosphere of the workplace will either motivate people or switch them off from doing their best. We also know that a large part of the variance in climate depends on the behaviour of the individual manager. That is to say the manager's style. The manager's ability to use a variety of styles appropriately depends to a large extent on his or her own competencies. So managing discretionary effort to enhance performance means the manager has to learn to read situations correctly and to manage his or her own behaviour to match the needs of the situation and create the kind of climate in which people will be motivated to do their best.

Hay/McBer make the proposition that there are four key factors which affect organisational/individual performance: personal characteristics, skills and motives; job requirements; managerial styles; and organisational climate (see Figure 10.1).

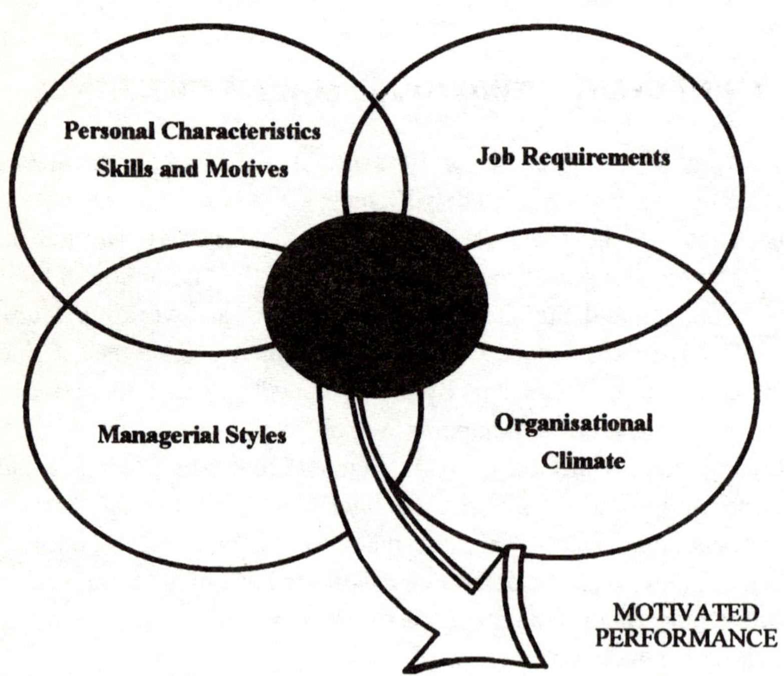

Figure 10.1 *Key factors affecting organisational/individual performance*

In this chapter we will focus particularly on the interaction of managerial styles/behaviours and workplace climates in the context of a performance management process.

The introduction of 'mixed model' performance management processes into team-based empowered organisations requires that all managers have to possess and demonstrate managerial behaviours which reinforce, not block, these processes and ensure that individuals/teams perform in motivating work climates.

MANAGERIAL BEHAVIOURS WHICH BUILD MOTIVATING CLIMATES

The performance management process is designed to encourage open, ongoing communication between employees and managers about performance matters. The process should be continuous, planful, participative and empowering. The philosophy of performance management is influenced strongly by the belief that it is a core management process involving the definition of the 'what' and 'how' of performance, monitoring, coaching and assessing. It is clearly concerned with basic aspects of 'good management practice'.

However, the behaviours and skills required of managers to be effective in the performance management process are often underestimated and misunderstood. To manage performance effectively managers need to know how to:

- ❑ define performance expectations
  (setting SMART objectives, understanding competencies);
- ❑ communicate with their staff
  (presentation skills);
- ❑ create a motivating environment
  (influence strategies, visionary leadership);
- ❑ coach employees;
- ❑ assess performance
  (both objectives and competencies, listening/feedback skills);
- ❑ give advice on performance improvements;

- ❑ confront poor performance;
- ❑ reinforce good performance.

To achieve an effective performance management culture requires a new style of 'enabling' managers with a range of skills involving the softer skills like motivation, empowerment, coaching and communication. Shedding the traditional 'command and control' model for one of 'lead and enable' is a most difficult transition for many managers. Managerial decision making must soften. Work may become more self-managed but it still has to 'managed' in different ways. Managers must still periodically review progress towards the objectives and coach the employees to even better performance. Successful managers will be masters at getting people to work effectively together, managing the work environment and networks and being effective coaches. Knowledge of the content of the job will no longer be the overriding requisite for promotion. The managers will 'add value' to their team by creating a climate in which the team feels empowered and is enabled to deliver high levels of performance.

Example

Here is a case from the US which illustrates how a healthcare company tried to change managerial behaviours through a new performance management process.

In a Regional Health System in South Carolina (USA) a new competency-based performance management process was introduced to replace a traditional performance appraisal system which was described by the chief executive as typical of most hospitals:

> Our reviews usually were two hour sessions at the end of the year, linked to pay, with nothing in between. Usually these kind of reviews only captured the last two months of activity. A lot was stored up during the year that was not getting expressed appropriately.

The company introduced a planning-coaching-review model in which the interactive, ongoing aspects were seen as one of its strongest points. Managers and subordinates were expected to plan together; there was to be at least one formal coaching session during the year; and the end of year review was no longer to be the one-way dialogue from manager to subordinate – it had to be a participative, subordinate-led discussion. 'I think there is a direct correlation between the amount of time a manager (actively) listens to an employee and the behavioural changes that result,' says the chief executive. One manager recently told me that in his review sessions 'I used to be talking 75 per cent of the time; now I am listening 80 per cent of the time.'

If employees feel they are in a trusting environment they will open up; if they feel attacked they will shut down. How managers behave towards their employees will largely determine how the employees react to the work environment.

WHAT IS ORGANISATIONAL CLIMATE?

The goal of effective performance management is to create an organisational climate in which employees will want to strive continuously for performance improvement. Using the weather as a metaphor, climate can be defined as 'the atmosphere of the workplace' or the answer to the question 'what is it like to work here?' It is a complex mixture of people's perceptions, expectations, policies and procedures that summarise 'the way we do things around here'.

Climate is important because:

- it affects individual and organisational performance, by arousing (or discouraging) motivation and commitment of the people in the organisation;
- its measurement gives management a reading on how well parts of the organisation are integrated, in the eyes of the employees;
- managers can greatly influence the organisational climate by their managerial styles.

The Primary Dimensions of Organisational Climate

There are six primary dimensions in the Hay/McBer model of organisational climate. The definitions of these six climate dimensions are:

1. **Flexibility**: The extent to which unnecessary procedures, policies and formality are minimised, and the extent to which people feel encouraged to develop new ideas and approaches.
2. **Responsibility**: The extent to which people in the work unit feel free to make decisions on their own about how they will do their jobs and the extent to which calculated risk taking is encouraged.
3. **Standards**: The extent to which people perceive the way management sets high standards and challenging goals and pushes people to improve their performance.
4. **Rewards**: The extent to which the allocation of rewards is perceived to be based on excellent performance, and the extent to which recognition and praise outweigh threats and criticism.
5. **Clarity**: The extent to which people are clear about procedures, expectations, and plans for the work group or organisation.
6. **Team Commitment**: The extent to which co-workers like and trust one another and cooperate, share information and resources, and help one another get the job done; the extent to which people will provide extra effort when needed, and the extent to which they feel proud to belong to the work unit or organisation.

These dimensions can be measured using organisational climate surveys, and changed through the use of different managerial behaviours. In a recent research paper Steve Kelner, Christine Rivers and Kathleen O'Connell[1] confirmed the strength of the link between managerial styles and organisational climate. It is based on an analysis of 3871 employees (managers, senior managers and executives). What was revealing was the degree to which the data showed that managerial styles correlate with climate variables and that a greater number of styles correlate with a higher (more productive) climate.

The plus and minus signs indicated in Table 10.1 refer to positive and negative correlations; zeros reflect the few occasions where ambiguous or zero correlations were expected. What the authors concluded from this information is that a manager who carries a range of styles in his/her 'pocket', and makes use of these styles at the appropriate times, creates a better climate. Though there are no 'good' or 'bad' styles the research indicates that the four positive correlating styles (authoritative, affiliative, democratic and coaching) are likely to be useful in most situations, while the two negative correlates (coercive and pacesetting) should be applied only in specific situations.

The research data indicate that style is heavily weighted on climate; in other words, a manager's behaviour and the way that behaviour is used in various situations accounts for more than half of the work climate that employees experience.

Table 10.1 *The link between managerial styles and organisational climate*

	MANAGERIAL STYLES					
CLIMATE DIMENSIONS	COERC.	AUTH.	AFF.	DEMO.	PACE.	COACH.
Flexibility	-	+	+	+	-	+
Responsibility	-	+	+	+	0	0
Standards	0	+	+	+	-	+
Rewards	-	+	+	+	-	+
Clarity	-	+	+	+	-	+
Commitment	-	+	+	+	-	+

Note: Actual data are found in original paper: *Managerial Style as a Predictor of Organisational Climate*

Let's look at the case of Richard, a training manager in a manufacturing company.

A climate survey was carried out using questionnaires with his staff. The results are shown in Figure 10.2.

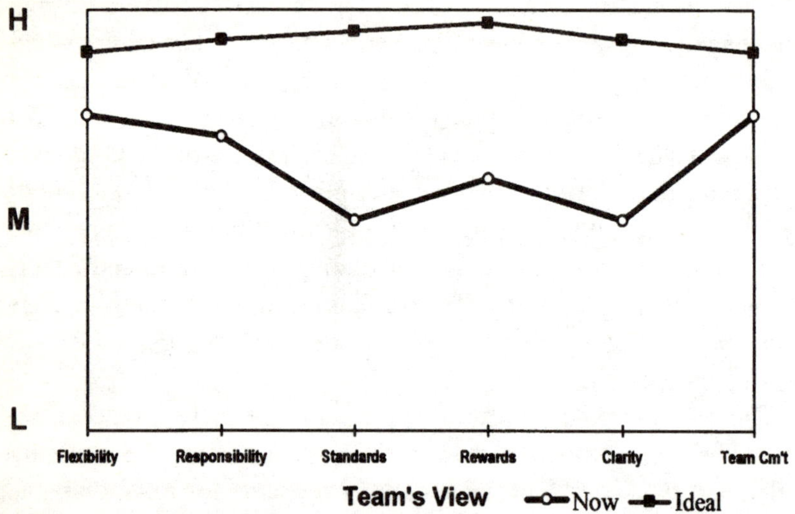

Figure 10.2 *Workplace climate (Richard)*

Richard manages a team of ten people. He likes training, enjoys his job, and is interested in people. The climate survey reveals significant gaps (between the present situation and the ideal situation) particularly in the four dimensions of standards, clarity, responsibility and rewards. There is a relatively good fit on flexibility and team commitment.

A look at Richard's management style profile gives us a real insight into this climate survey (Figure 10.3).

What does this profile tell us about the way Richard manages his team? First an explanation of each 'style':

- ❑ *Coercive*: the 'do it the way I tell you' manager who closely controls subordinates and motivates by threats and discipline.
- ❑ ***Authoritative***: the 'firm but fair' manager who gives subordinates clear direction and motivates by persuasion and feedback on task performance.
- ❑ ***Affiliative***: the 'people first, task second' manager who emphasises good relationships among subordinates and motivates by trying to keep people happy with fringe benefits, security and social activities.

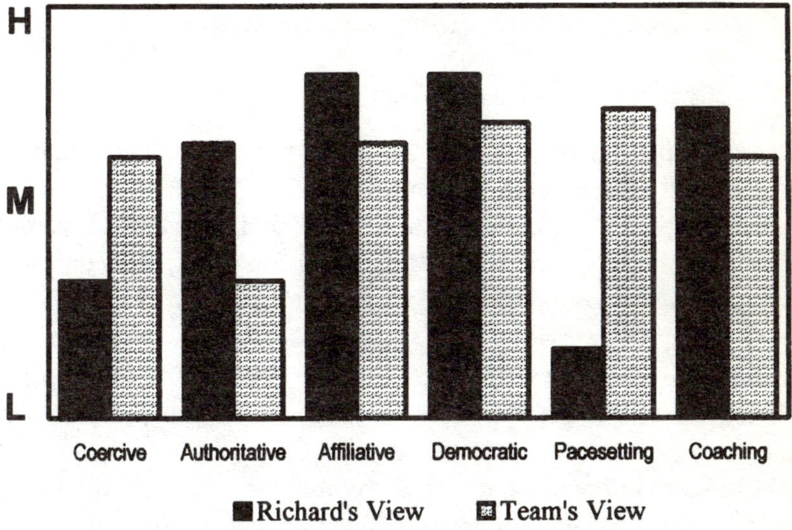

Figure 10.3 *Management style (Richard)*

- ❑ ***Democratic***: the 'participative' manager who encourages subordinate input in decision making and motivates by rewarding team effort.
- ❑ ***Pacesetting***: the 'do it myself' manager who performs many tasks personally, expects subordinates to follow his or her example, and motivates by setting and demanding high standards of work.
- ❑ ***Coaching***: the 'developmental' manager who helps and encourages subordinates to improve their performance, and motivates by providing opportunities for professional development.

From the profile, it is clear that Richard's team regarded his styles as being:

High:	Affiliative.
Medium:	Coercive, democratic, pacesetting (medium/ high), coaching.
Low:	Authoritative.

Whereas Richard regarded his styles as being:

Medium/High: Affiliative, democratic, coaching.
Medium: Authoritative.
Low: Coercive, pacesetting.

This combination of styles creates a workplace climate which is very friendly but lacking in clear direction. The staff lack clarity about what they are expected to achieve and to what standards. They don't know where they are going and don't know how they are doing. If they encounter a problem Richard is likely to solve it for them (pacesetting style), probably because he wants to help them (affiliative style). There is little coaching going on. It is a warm, friendly place but not a climate in which significant performance improvements will be made.

In order to improve the workplace climate so that it is more motivating, Richard needs to close the gaps – particularly on the four dimension of standards, clarity, responsibility and rewards. He can do this by developing two managerial styles – authoritative and coaching – and by applying them more frequently and regularly through the performance management cycle.

The key phases of the performance management process can each have a significant impact on the climate dimensions of standards, clarity, responsibility and rewards (Figure 10.4).

To increase standards

1. Research shows that employees who are highly motivated to obtain their objectives are those who are working towards challenging, yet realistic, goals. In the performance planning phase it is essential to develop key objectives that are stretching for each employee. This requires an understanding of each employee's capabilities, since what may be stretching for one, may not be stretching for another.

   One must be careful not to set objectives so stretching that they become unrealistic. It is important to identify with the employee what factors could get in the way of achieving each objective.

Figure 10.4 *Key phases of the performance management process*

2. During the coaching phase discussions should take place aimed to motivate employees to strive towards high standards and stretching objectives. Any gaps in performance must be identified and action plans prepared. It is not sensible to automatically revise the objectives in order to make them easier to achieve. This will send a message that your standards are not high. The theme should be 'constant improvement'.

3. In the performance review it is important to remind employees that they will be assessed on the objectives that they have/have not met and the competencies they have/have not demonstrated. High ratings should not be given lightly.

   Employees need to understand and appreciate that high ratings are difficult (though not impossible) to receive.

Promoting high standards can also impact the next year's planning by enabling managers and employees to agree jointly to increase effective employees' expectations.

So the specific actions Richard can take to increase the standards dimension are:

- ❑ jointly set stretching yet realistic objectives with his staff;
- ❑ focus on continuous improvement of performance;
- ❑ identify actions needed to overcome potential/actual obstacles to meeting objectives;
- ❑ coach employees throughout the year;
- ❑ communicate standards expected and model them in his performance;
- ❑ do not tolerate mediocrity or lower standards;
- ❑ give periodic feedback (positive and negative) on employee performance.

To increase clarity

1. Employees need to understand the 'big picture', ie the organisation's vision, values and business strategy. This provides a framework in which they can think about and determine their own contribution to the organisation's success.

   The development of individual key objectives/expectations is a way of linking up the employee to the wider organisation. The setting of objectives should provide a clear focus for their efforts and energies.

   The objectives themselves should not be ambiguous. The usual test is that a good objective should be **S.M.A.R.T. (s):**

S pecific
M easurable
A chievable
R ealistic
T ime Related
(Stretching)

The performance planning discussion between manager and employee should provide clarity of direction and focus and a set of key objectives/expectations on which there is complete agreement and understanding.

2. During the year there should be periodic discussions to check progress against objectives and to clarify any misunderstandings and problems encountered. They are opportunities to restate the priorities and to re-emphasise the importance of the employee's contribution to the organisation's strategy.
3. The annual performance review discussion should clarify the extent to which the employee has achieved his/her objectives. If coaching discussions have taken place throughout the year, employees will have a deeper understanding of what has been achieved and how performance could be improved during the next year.

So to increase the clarity dimension, Richard should hold:

- ❑ regular briefing sessions with his team to communicate the business strategy of the company, how this impacts on the team and what are his objectives for the year;
- ❑ performance planning discussions with each employee to draw up and agree (jointly) the employee's objectives for the year;
- ❑ periodic progress reviews during the year with each employee (Richard will be in the coaching style);
- ❑ an annual performance review with each employee.

To increase responsibility

1. Responsibility is about encouraging and enabling employees to take ownership of their own performance objectives. Empowering them to take decisions which will enable them to

reach objectives is crucial. Thus Richard has to create a climate in which individuals can feel relaxed about taking their own decisions and even occasionally making mistakes without always having a 'fear of failure'. Team members should be encouraged to try out new ways of performing their work wherever possible.

Understanding the importance of their key objectives (and recognising that others are dependent upon them to achieve them) will help employees understand how and where to prioritise their time. This has got to apply to managers too, who have to understand the importance of creating time themselves to manage the performance of their team throughout the year. In other words performance management has got to be a priority for managers. But if they develop the climate dimension of responsibility each employee will be taking a large measure of ownership of their performance from the manager.

2. During the year the employee should be encouraged to plan for the progress reviews and coaching discussions. The effective coach does not take over the employee's problems (that is a pacesetting style); he will empower the employee to problem-solve and find solutions to their problems, with support and advice from the coach as required.

   So Richard needs to develop his coaching style and to apply it continuously through the performance management cycle. His employees need to be encouraged and empowered to take an equal share in managing their performance throughout the year and in assessing their own performance at the end of the year.
3. Employees should be empowered to take responsibility for their own performance review discussions. Employees (in partnership with their managers) need to track their performance, identify trends and take corrective action, throughout the year.

A performance management process which is operated on these principles will have a significant impact on the 'responsibility' dimension of the workplace climate.

So what are the actions Richard could take in order to increase the responsibility dimension?

- ❑ he needs to be less pacesetting and develop a coaching style for more situations;
- ❑ he should create an atmosphere of trust in which employees want to take on more ownership and responsibility for their own performance:
  - ask employees to draft objectives and plan the review meetings;
  - encourage innovative objectives and do not punish risk taking;
  - ask employees to prepare action plans for achievement of key objectives and for overcoming any obstacles encountered during the year.

To increase rewards

The concept of rewards goes beyond financial returns. Creating a positive atmosphere in which employees feel valued and recognised for their contributions is critically important. Intangible rewards, like providing social recognition and words of praise, are within a manager's control. Therefore rewarding behaviour is an ongoing managerial activity, not just an annual pay-linked ritual.

1. Employees need to know how 'good' performance will be rewarded, and if there are links between performance and pay, what they are and how they operate. They should have a clear idea of the factors which are to be rewarded – whether it is the achievement of key objectives or demonstration of competencies or a combination of both.
2. In the ongoing review discussions the employee's self-esteem has got to be reinforced. Positive reinforcement of 'what has gone well' will help greatly. These discussions should be about recognising what has been achieved and agreeing how performance could be improved in future years.

   Employees who have met their objectives can be encouraged to take on a mentoring role for their colleagues and/or take on extra responsibilities. It is essential to get away from the 'blame cultures' which prevail in many organisations. While in a proper performance culture it is not appropriate to reward employees who have not met their performance expectations, it is possible to acknowledge the difficulties they might have faced and the efforts they have made to overcome them.

3. After a performance review discussion Richard's employees should feel a sense of pride in their accomplishments and a desire to improve their developmental areas. Treating employees with respect and helping them plan for performance improvements is a far better way of rewarding them than criticising or attaching blame.

By focusing on the four climate dimensions of standards, clarity, responsibility and rewards, Richard would be able to improve the overall workplace climate. By emphasising these four dimensions Richard will also help to maximise the other two climate dimensions: flexibility and team commitment. Here is how:

- High clarity ensures high flexibility because a recognition of the difficulty with which certain goals could be accomplished in the organisation during the previous year may require a strategic change in planning for the next year's key objectives and competency expectations. Creating a more open and trusting climate in which employees are encouraged to innovate and expand their jobs will increase flexibility also.
- Responsibility for planning for the performance review discussions entails open communications between employees in order to track their performance. The performance management process encourages employees to work cooperatively and to be aware of the high level of dependence on one another. This openness and more collaborative working, as well as the feeling of equity which results from everyone being part of the same performance management process, will result in a higher team commitment.

THE IMPORTANCE OF COACHING

While it is important to stress that all six managerial styles have their place (depending on the job/job holder/situation) it is clear that *coaching* is critically important for the effective management of employees' performance. Coaching is the continuous process in which manager and employee engage in constructive dialogue about past and future performance. As a key practice for improving performance it helps to shape behaviours throughout the year and narrow the gaps between actual and expected performance. It is often underdeveloped in appraisal training.

What are the qualities of good coaches? Perhaps you can think of someone who helps you in a leisure interest – like tennis, yoga, bridge, cookery or foreign languages, or a coach of national or international standing – like football coaches or choreography teachers with the Royal Ballet? Whoever it is in your mind, they are likely to share the following characteristics:

- ❑ ***Genuine***: the quality of being available, open and honest with others. It is reflected in sincere interest in helping to solve problems, learn new technology and improve skills.
- ❑ ***Empowering***: having positive expectations that people can do well without doing all the work for them. This means that good coaches help people identify how to solve their work problems without the manager providing all the answers – or even taking over aspects of their work.
- ❑ ***Understanding***: this is the ability to understand an employee's work problems. The coach must be attentive, insightful, sensitive and open minded. It reflects their capacity to be flexible, adaptable and probing.
- ❑ ***Analytical/problem solving***: the ability to diagnose where performance is falling short of standards required and to offer appropriate advice/assistance which brings about performance improvements.

They will also have a clearer understanding too of their own role as enablers rather than controllers: that is a pretty healthy change. They will have much more confidence to manage that role rather than trying to lead from the front all the time.

Will Richard be able to develop these coaching qualities? First we must look at the competencies which help team leaders become more effective coaches and then compare Richard's competency profile (Figure 10.5) with them.

❑ **Interpersonal sensitivity**
- Understands both strengths and limitations of employees.
- Understands the reasons for employees' behaviour.
- Knows what motivates individual employees as well as what turns them off.
- Takes the time to listen to employees' problems.

❑ **Developing others**
- Gives employees assignments or training to develop them.
- Gives encouragement and open praise to employees to improve their motivation.
- Gives employees specific, detailed feedback.

❑ **Team management**
- Ensures that all employees contribute to team goals.
- Gives recognition to employees who have contributed to the team's success.
- Sets an example and encourages employees to develop an atmosphere of teamwork and cooperation.
- Pushes for solutions to conflict in which the individuals and the group as a whole benefit.

❑ **Self confidence**
- Approaches employees with a positive 'can-do' attitude.
- Is secure in his/her own judgement and at the same time receptive to employees' ideas.
- Expresses opinions and gives feedback to employees confidently without arrogance or hostility.

❑ **Self control**
- Remains calm in stressful situations.
- Refrains from impulsive reactions or behaviours that would interfere with a motivating relationship with employees.
- Keeps calm and constructive in the face of employees' anger.

❑ **Use of concepts**
- Uses past experience and observations to understand and help handle employees' present working challenges.
- Relates employees' performance objectives to key values and strategies of the organisation.

❑ **Analytical thinking**
- Analyses employee behaviour to determine underlying causes.
- Accurately anticipates the consequences of his/her own behaviour towards employees.
- Uses systematic approach to handling employee challenges.
- Anticipates obstacles in seeking to develop employees.

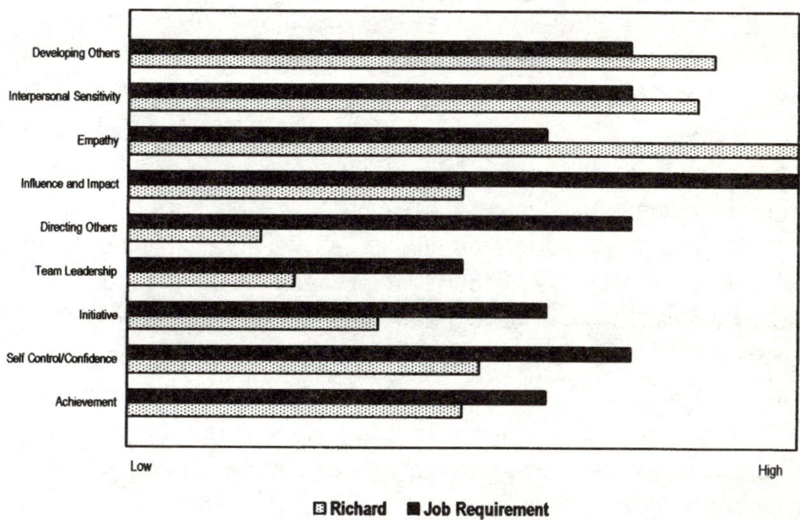

Figure 10.5 *Competency profile (Richard)*

From Richard's competency profile (Figure 10.5) we know that he meets (or exceeds) job requirements on:

- ❑ Developing others
- ❑ Interpersonal sensitivity
- ❑ Empathy.

but does not meet job requirements on:

- ❑ Influence and impact
- ❑ Directing others
- ❑ Team leadership
- ❑ Initiative
- ❑ Self control/confidence.

On this evidence, in order to further develop his coaching qualities Richard has to develop his team leadership and self confidence competencies. The other competencies which need to be developed, ie influence and impact, directing others and initiative, will improve his authoritative style.

SUMMARY

This chapter has emphasised the critical importance of using the performance management process to create a motivating climate for all employees. It is clear that managerial behaviours do have a significant impact on workplace climate. So to improve climate requires changes in managerial behaviours. Managers have got to have well developed directing and supportive styles in order to add value to their teams. The performance management process – if properly enacted – will have a major impact on workplace climate, particularly in the dimensions of standards, clarity, responsibility and rewards. It is clear that a continuous coaching style combined with occasional periods of 'firm but fair' leadership is the most likely to give employees the motivating climate in which they will want to improve their performance.

Reference

1. Kelner, S; Rivers, C; O'Connell, K (1993) *Management Styles as a Behavioural Predictor of Organisational Climate* McBer, Boston

Chapter 11

Self-Managed Individuals and Teams

THE MOVE TOWARDS SELF-MANAGEMENT

According to the *Economist*[1], *Fortune*, a business magazine, estimates that half of America's large companies are experimenting with self-managing teams. A new paternalism is sweeping the boardrooms and shop floors. Motorola, a chips to cellphone company, earmarks more than $100 million a year for training, with everyone in the company spending at least a week a year back in the classroom, courtesy of the company. Levi Strauss, a clothing manufacturer, invites its workers to redesign key parts of the production process. Procter and Gamble reports that productivity is up to 40 per cent higher in plants that use team-based production. It seems that delayering and creating empowered teams and individuals is taking place not only in the innovative fast-moving sectors but also in the larger, more conservative organisations (which would fit comfortably in the functional work culture).

All organisations are being subjected to similar pressures for change and are moving towards developing and creating more empowered teams/individuals.

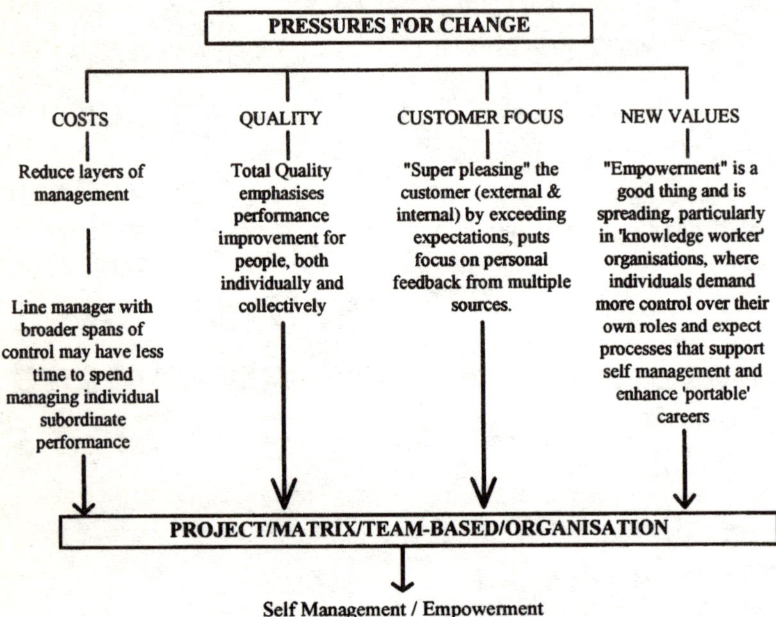

Figure 11.1 *The move towards self-management*

Today's organisations are having to change too rapidly to expect only managers to have the answers.

Cook and Macauley[2] make the important point that

> self-management is not easy. It requires both time and effort both on the part of employees and the employer. It does not bring instant results, but it does facilitate a learning environment where individuals are encouraged to take responsibility for their personal contribution and development. This in turn creates a sense of empowerment.

The Commission on the Skills of the American Workforce has observed that the most productive organisations worldwide are doing away with the traditional top-down management of hierarchies and bureaucracy and replacing this with self-managing work teams. This is happening in Ford, Rover Group, Shell, Citicorp, IBM, Kodak, Motorola, Procter and Gamble, Rank Xerox and many others.

As organisations get flatter, less hierarchical, more empowering and the managerial accountabilities are spread out among fewer people, the concept of self-management becomes increasingly important. Individuals and teams have to take on a greater role in managing their performance within a looser, less prescriptive corporate framework.

'Self management' is an important principle which underpins effective performance management. I have argued in earlier chapters for the need to develop line manager ownership of the performance management process but performance management is not a process which should be driven solely by managers. It has to be felt and operated as a two-way process at the very minimum. With flatter, more flexible team-based organisations more people will inevitably be drawn into the heart of the process, eg peers, colleagues, customers. Inevitably the trend of performance management is to give employees more control of the process both in terms of its design, its implementation and its evolution.

However, changing structures and processes is one thing; changing behaviours and attitudes is altogether a more difficult task. Creating and sustaining self-managed teams (and individuals) is a harder task than it sounds. As Tom Peters has said, 'oddly enough, it's managers who are having the toughest time making the shift. Well it's not so odd, on second thoughts. Many of their jobs are disappearing.'

Managing in these new environments requires different managerial skills. In de-layered organisations there are less people about to be 'managers'. These people have to change how they manage or they will burn out. They have to be more 'visionary' and authoritative, ie provide direction, vision, stretching goals and less 'hands-on'. They have to understand how they add value – by creating the kind of positive work climate which enables their 'customers' – ie their subordinates and colleagues – to meet their needs and deliver high levels of performance. In flatter, empowered organisations managers have got to show strong leadership and coaching skills and they have got to be prepared to let go. A team manager in an insurance company which introduced empowered team working sums it up nicely: 'the hardest thing was to hand over to someone else and trust them to do it as well as I would.' As in other empowered workplaces the team manager or supervisor no longer commands and controls: he or she coaches, discusses and assesses training needs.

A LOOK THROUGH YOUR WINDOW

One of the most accessible tools of self-awareness is the *Johari Window* (Fig. 11.2). It provides a focus to examine where self-awareness can be improved.

SELF		
	Known to you	**Unknown to you**
Known to others	The public you	The blind spot
Unknown to others	The private you	Area of potential

Figure 11.2 *The Johari Window*

It is a useful framework for exploring and extending self-awareness. It uses two dimensions and two divisions of these dimensions to describe you; what is known and what is unknown to you: what is known and unknown by others. There are four 'window panes' which you and other people can look through.

There is our public face, the one we show to customers and colleagues. How do you come across? Have you ever asked for any feedback? Sometimes other people will see you differently from the way you see yourself and you may be unaware of this. This is your 'blind spot'.

There are things that you naturally wish to keep to yourself, particularly in a work context. This is 'the private you'. However, if you are too much of a closed book, other people may see you as aloof or unwelcoming or disapproving. Equally, being inappropriately open can unsettle a working relationship.

The area of potential is the area of *unknown* potential! The aim must be to increase your self-knowledge and reduce this hidden area. So getting feedback about yourself from others is very important in any 'self-managed' environment. The most effective way to find out how others see you is to ask them. Feedback is essential. It gives a greater sense of self-respect and self-knowledge through reinforcement of good performance and greater understanding of shortcomings. Feedback gives us the chance to improve, rather than repeating the same mistakes all over again.

PERFORMANCE MANAGEMENT THROUGH SELF-MANAGEMENT

Hay Management Consultants has developed a model of change and improvement based on the principle of self-managed performance. The model can be applied to individuals and teams. There are six steps in the cycle (see Figure 11.3).

Steps 1 and 2: Self-awareness

Self-awareness

Where am I going?
What will success look like?
Where am I now?
Where are the gaps?

The first two steps in the cycle involve an iteration, based around self-knowledge and self-awareness, but in the context of what the organisation needs from the individual/team. It is a process of self-diagnosis, data collection and analysis, drawing on internal and external 'stakeholder' sources. Templates need to be developed, to define both *what* has to be achieved and *how* it can be achieved.

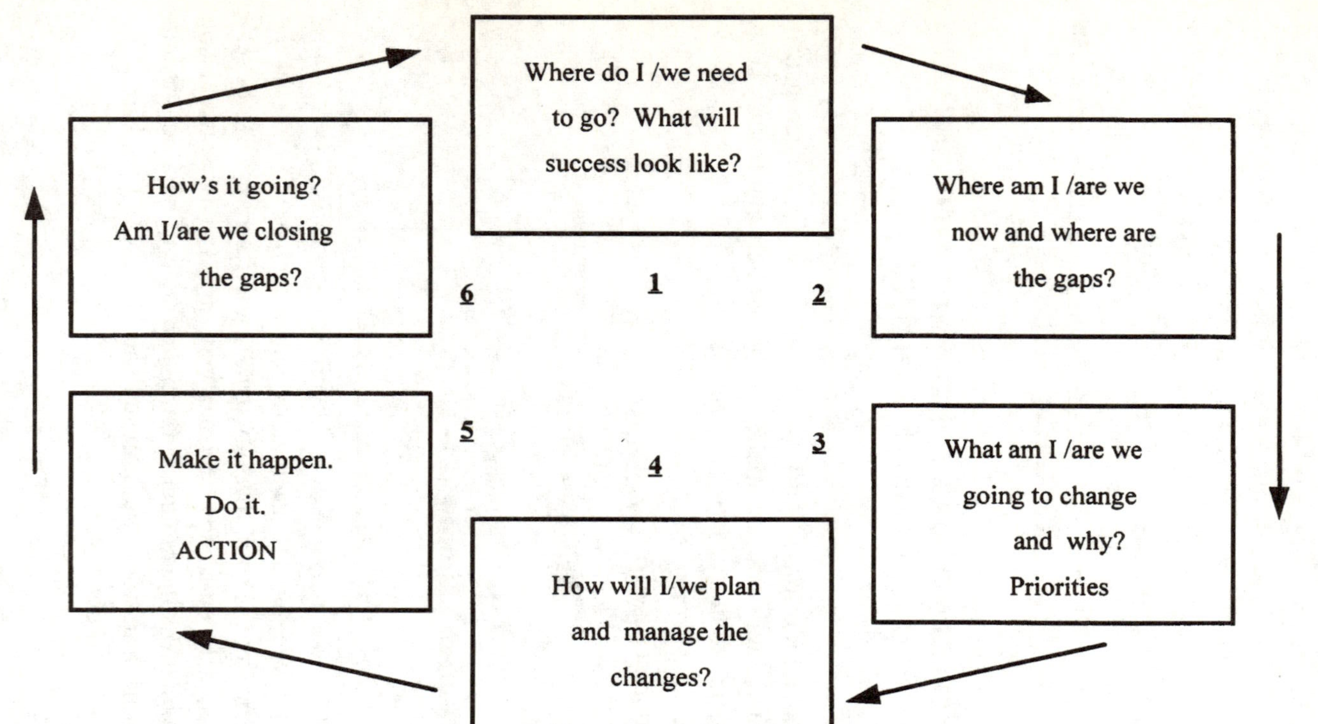

Figure 11.3 *Self-managed performance: a model of change and improvement*

Step 3: Establishing priorities

Establishing priorities

What am I going to change and why?
Priorities?

The first two steps involved bringing together relevant data to carry out a gap analysis, in order to increase self-awareness. This process should help the individual/team improve their understanding of the need for change, by creating tension between where they need to be and where they are.

Step 3 in the cycle requires a commitment to change, by focusing on a limited number of 'gaps', with a clear rationale for why these should be the priorities. The process has to be supported by a clear set of criteria for choosing which gaps to close. Establishing and applying the most appropriate criteria is central to successful performance management, as it involves a 'trade off' between what the organisation needs and what the individual/team needs.

The individual/team has to obtain 'sign off' to these priorities from the various stakeholders, which requires significant influencing competencies.

Step 4: Action planning

Action planning

How will I plan
and manage
the changes?

This step involves the production of a performance plan, which can also embrace a self-development and learning plan. Whether this is formally written down or not, its content needs to be communicated to the stakeholders, team colleagues and other partners, so that they understand:

- what the individual/team intends to achieve and their action plans;
- how this fits in with their own plans and needs;
- what support they need to provide to the individual/team, if the plan is to be achieved;
- how implementation and progress of the plan will be managed and monitored by the individual/team and others.

Step 5: Implementation and action

Implementation and action

How do I/we implement the plans?
What Support Network do I/we need?

Step 5 in the cycle is about implementation of the performance plans through action. The individual/team needs to assemble and manage their own support network of people, who will provide feedback, encouragement, coaching and counselling throughout the plan period. No one person is likely to have all the knowledge, skills and competencies required for this support – in particular the line manager may be the least appropriate person to focus this support.

Several support networks may have to be integrated by the individuals:

- Functional, professional development for career purposes.
- Project management, for progressing each task.
- Customer/client partnerships, for ensuring 'satisfaction'.
- Team networks, for local geographical support.

Step 6: Performance reviews

> **Performance reviews**
>
> How am I/we doing?
> Am I closing the gaps?
> Who has valid evidence/feedback?

This final step involves the periodic review of performance against the agreed performance plan. The organisation's processes may dictate that the individual/team undertake specific milestone reviews, to check on progress and to evaluate levels of achievement. These could be part of a project team management process, customer satisfaction review, functional team review etc.

The individual/team must ensure that review mechanisms are in place and applied, with respect to the priority areas. These may operate on different timescales, from daily to annually.

There should be self-review processes involving data collection, analysis and learning on a 360 degree basis, from all the key stakeholders around the individual/team.

The individual/team may look to one or more other people, to help with the formal periodic assessment of achievement and learning, both in terms of data selection, analysis, interpretation and overall judgement.

THE SKILLS FOR SELF-MANAGEMENT

In the UK the National Council for Vocational Qualifications has developed a skills framework for self-managing individuals (Table 11.1).

Table 11.1 *NCVQ skills framework for improving own learning and performance*

LEVEL 1	1.1	Contribute to the process of identifying strengths and weaknesses and agree short-term targets. *Performance criteria:* 1 the accuracy of own understanding of targets is confirmed with person setting them; 2 information relevant to accurate identification of strengths and weaknesses is provided on request; 3 information provided is based on appropriate evidence.
	1.2	Follow given activities to learn and to improve performance. *Performance criteria:* 1 agreed schedule of activities is followed; 2 targets are met; 3 support from others is used effectively.
LEVEL 2		
LEVEL 3	3.1	Identify strengths and weaknesses and contribute to the process of identifying short-term targets. *Performance criteria:* 1 the accuracy of own understanding of targets is confirmed with person setting them; 2 information relevant to accurate identification of strengths and weaknesses is provided on request; 3 information provided is based on appropriate evidence; 4 information relevant to targets is provided on request.
	3.2	Seek and make use of feedback, follow given activities to learn and to improve performance. *Performance criteria:* 1 agreed schedule of activities is followed; 2 targets are met; 3 support from others is used effectively; 4 changes recommended are implemented promptly; 5 feedback is treated constructively;

	6 difficulties encountered are brought promptly to the attention of others; 7 feedback on performance and progress is actively and regularly sought.
LEVEL 4	
LEVEL 5	5.1 Identify strengths and weaknesses and propose short and long-term targets. *Performance criteria:* 1 the accuracy of own understanding of targets is confirmed with person setting them; 2 information relevant to accurate identification of strengths and weaknesses is provided on request; 3 information provided is based on appropriate evidence; 4 information relevant to targets is provided on request; 5 targets proposed are appropriate and based on appropriate information; 6 strengths and weaknesses are identified accurately; 7 proposed targets are agreed and confirmed with others; 8 targets are reviewed regularly and revised in response to changing circumstances.
	5.2 Seek and make use of feedback, select and follow a wide range of activities to learn and to improve performance. *Performance criteria:* 1 agreed schedule of activities is followed; 2 targets are met; 3 support from others is used effectively; 4 changes recommended are implemented promptly; 5 feedback is treated constructively; 6 difficulties encountered are brought promptly to the attention of others; 7 feedback on performance and progress is actively and regularly sought;

		8 activities chosen to improve learning and performance are appropriate to the individual's strengths and weaknesses, and the context in which the individual is working.

SELF-MANAGING TEAMS

Various definitions have been advanced for self-managing work teams. Among them are:

> A work group allocated an overall task and given discretion over how the work is to be done. These groups are 'self-regulating' and work without direct supervision.[3]

> They represent the transfer of considerable authority down the corporate ladder. Teams have authority over 'doing things right' and 'doing right things'.[4]

Table 11.2 *Self-managing work teams*

Are teams doing *right* things?	**Are teams doing *things* right?**
1. What are the organisation's values, structure and culture? How do they link with its goals and vision for the future?	8. Teams working on district issues (or, if overlap, are boundaries clear)?
2. What kind of teams exist/should exist? How do they link with the the organisation's strategic goals?	9. Senior management clearing obstacles?
3. Issues linked to strategic goals?	10. Teams charted? Clearly? Executive sponsors clear on parameters, expectations, target measures, time frames that define expectations of the teams?
4. Issues key to improving daily work?	11. Teams led by effective team leaders? Team leaders fulfilling their responsibility?
5. Issues clearly defined? – Important/high profile? – Cross-functional? – Process-related? – Big impact – Unusual/difficult?	12. Working with trained facilitators? Effectively?

Are teams doing *right* things?	Are teams doing *things* right?
6. Interconnection of teams clear to senior management? – Important/high profile? – Rest of organisations? 7. Interconnecting of teams with natural work groups?	13. Teams properly staffed? – Working with effective meeting? – Managing team dynamics? – Properly motivated? Supported as individuals by their natural work groups?

From the definitions in Table 11.2 we can see that self-managing teams are relatively small, highly autonomous work groups that take complete responsibility for a product, project or service. By empowering the workers with the authority to shape the destiny of their group, many organisations are discovering that employees actually possess a great deal of hidden potential which can be used to advance the competitiveness of the firm. Research indicates that organisations which encourage employee self-management can increase productivity by some 30 per cent.[5]

What makes teams work effectively?

Richard Bechard,[6] in his now classic model of team effectiveness, defined the factors that influence team performance:

- ❑ setting *goals* or priorities;
- ❑ how work is allocated (*roles*);
- ❑ the way the team is working (*its processes*); and
- ❑ the *relationships* among the people doing the work.

The shape and make-up of the four factors will reflect the work cultures which prevail in the organisation. Hay/McBer's approach to team effectiveness is shown in Figure 11.4.

What behavioural competencies are required for team-based success?

In the UK a major road construction company embarked on a large scale programme to change culture and improve performance

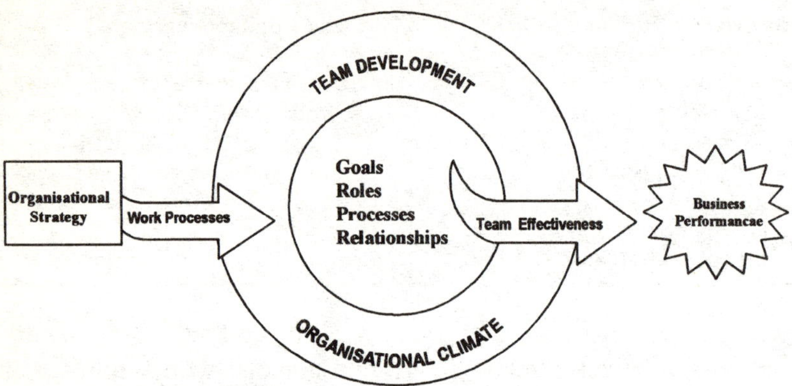

Figure 11.4 *Team effectiveness (Hay/McBer)*

through a stronger team-based organisation. As part of its newly-devised human resource strategy, it recognised the need to build upon what was good in the old culture but to discard that which was backward-looking and obstructive. In particular, it identified the need to place greater emphasis on individual contribution and performance, but through a team-based organisation. Team skills became of greater relevance and importance and one of nine competencies against which each employee is reviewed. How the company defines the team skills competency is set out in the box below.

TEAM SKILLS

Definition
The ability to work and cooperate willingly with others, both in own work team and other working groups.

Explanation
This competency is concerned with the way in which the employee behaves in groups. Factors to consider are the degree to which the employee helps and supports colleagues; the contribution the employee makes to the team; the sacrifices and compromises the employee makes on behalf on the team; flexibility to undertake different roles within the team.

		Behavioural indicators
Excellent:	Always contributes to the team's performance and actively seeks to promote the team and improve its workings.	❑ Can adopt different team roles. ❑ Puts interests of team before self. ❑ Inspires others to contribute. ❑ Reduces conflicts and builds cohesion in team.

Very Good:	Continually contributes positively to the team and helps improve its workings.	❑ Positively influences team performance. ❑ Identifies with other team members. ❑ Volunteers assistance to others. ❑ Encourages other team members.
Fully Acceptable:	Works and cooperates willingly with others in own work team and other work groups.	❑ Understands the team's objectives and priorities. ❑ Committed to team and its goals. ❑ Cooperative. ❑ Does their 'fair share'.
Reasonable:	Sometimes fails to work and cooperate willingly with others.	❑ Holds back from full participation. ❑ Can withdraw from the team. ❑ Limited contribution to team effort.
Unacceptable:	Unwilling to work with others, and uncooperative.	❑ Disruptive. ❑ Unenthusiastic. ❑ Insular. ❑ Puts self before team.

Of course, team leaders need additional competencies such as developing others and empowerment.

DEVELOPING OTHERS

Definition

Strives to improve the skills of subordinates or others by providing clear behaviourally specific performance feedback, effective coaching and mentoring, and development experiences and opportunities.

Behavioural indicators:

❑ Gives encouragement to others to improve their motivation.
❑ Reassures others after setbacks.
❑ Takes extra time to assist and provides specific, detailed follow-up.
❑ Devotes significant time to providing task-related help to others.
❑ Gives people assignments and training to develop their abilities.
❑ Gives others latitude to do tasks the way they want.

EMPOWERMENT

Definition:
Empowers individuals and groups by sharing responsibility so that they have a deep sense of commitment and ownership, participate and contribute at high levels, are creative and innovative, take sound risks and are willing to be held accountable, and demonstrate leadership.

Behavioural indicators:
- ❑ Delegates full authority and responsibility to appropriate employees with the latitude to do a task in their own way.
- ❑ Provides opportunities for others to make and learn from mistakes in a non-critical setting.
- ❑ Publicly credits others who have performed well.
- ❑ Accepts and supports others' considered views, recommendations, or actions.

MAKING SELF-MANAGEMENT WORK – THE CRITICAL SUCCESS FACTORS

It should be clear from previous chapters that performance management is a two-way process involving manager and subordinates in continuous joint dialogue throughout the performance management cycle. Thus a considerable amount of individual 'self-management' is critical to effective performance management. In all organisations it is a question of degree and balance. In truly empowered team-based organisations there is an even greater emphasis on 'self-management' by individuals and teams. So what are the critical success factors for effective performance management in such work environments?

Top direction/vision

- ❑ There have to be consistent strategies and policies across the organisation which emphasise and reinforce 'self-management' such as career planning, personal development and learning, 'freedom to act' within boundaries of defined roles.

- Senior managers have to be seen as 'role models' and to be demonstrating daily the self-managing values.

Business processes

- The business processes have got to reinforce the activities associated with the self-management cycle. Thus there should be clarity around organisation processes for business planning, project planning, resource allocation, plus cross-functional forums where performance plans are shared, aligned and supported.
- Training programmes should emphasise self-management skills and know-how.
- Recognition and reward processes should reinforce team and individual performance.

People competencies

- There should be clear templates for self-management competencies which are used for selection, development, progression and recognition.
- Equally there should be clear definitions for support characteristics, such as coaching, counselling and mentoring.

Culture and climate

- Management styles should emphasise the 'empowering' styles, ie affiliative, democratic and coaching.
- Information is easily available, showed and timely – as not a culture where 'information is power'.
- Lots of 'freedom to act' balanced by a major emphasis on delivery of results. Achievement drive is a core organisation competency.
- There is a networking culture, where different networks thrive (and wither) very much dependent on the enthusiasm and interest of specific individuals rather than entirely business driven.

Case study: A total performance management process in a management consultancy

An emphasis on self-management is particularly appropriate in organisations which contain 'knowledge workers', ie highly qualified professionals, who are likely to demand more control over their own jobs/roles, careers and development. They would expect processes that support self-management and enhance 'portable' careers.

In this case study we look at the performance management process in a major management consultancy, which contains over 120 highly qualified and extremely individualistic consultants.

Figure 11.5 shows a model which illustrates the process. The process is designed to improve performance as a basis for reward, training, development and succession planning. It is largely self-managed by the individual, although help and support are provided by others such as team leaders, colleagues, regional operations directors and project managers.

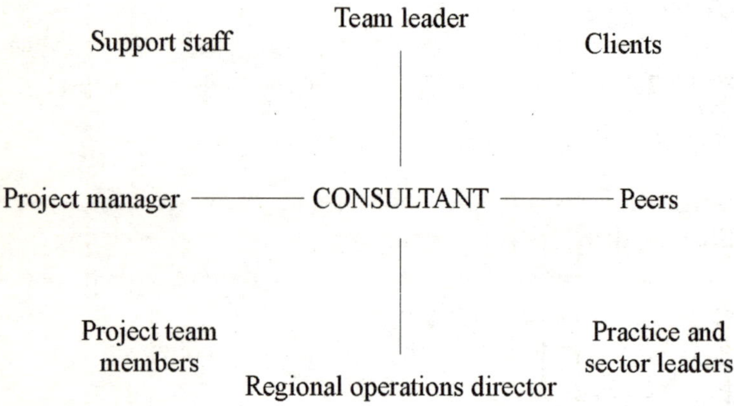

How the process works

1. Performance planning takes place between the regional operating director and the consultant. At least two formal meetings take place during the year to agree and subsequently revise a personal performance plan. During the meetings between them, attention will be focused on a number of areas:

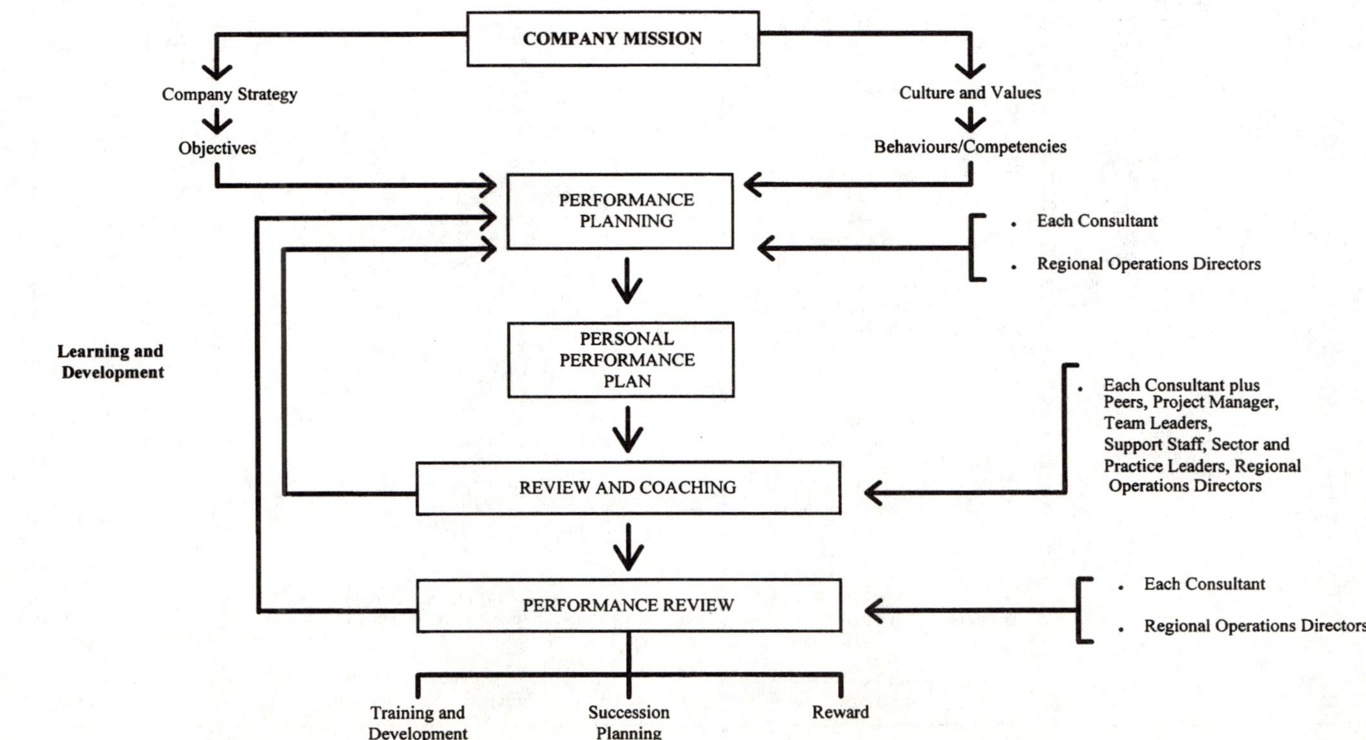

Figure 11.5 *The model of consultant development and performance improvement*

Table 11.3 Consultant personal performance plan 1993/94

Accountability	Measures of performance	Competencies	Individual goals
Performance in the market place	**Client relationship management**	**Client relationship management**	
Client relationship management	Clear, comprehensive client plans Evidence of good, active relationships – visits and file notes Development of additional points of entry Positioning of colleagues to match opportunities (practice, sector, team) Effective client plan monitoring and review Evidence of active marketing to clients (events, mailing, etc) Up-to-date client contact lists Use of client contact lists Use of clients for referral No complaints!	Focus on client needs Building personal partnerships with clients Interpersonal sensitivity/ awareness Presentation skills and use of influencing strategies Self control with clients Business appreciation, mindedness Pattern recognition Analytical thinking	
Support to team in marketing	**Marketing** Event organisation Other allocated roles Client/contact attendance Follow-up	**Initiative** Superior consultants show initiative particularly in overcoming obstacles. They recognise and seize opportunities They constantly scan their environment for information and act to create opportunites. **Business appreciation mindedness** This is an awareness and concern for business issues, processes and outcomes. Superior consultants will focus their consulting to meet clients' business needs.	
Sales performance	**Sales** Contribution to team CRM sales Individual contribution (sales credits)	**Innovation** This competency involves a mixture of achievement drive (waiting to do something new, willing to take a risk), the ability to spot patterns and opportunities within clients and then making the effort to focus these to meet client needs.	

   - performance in the market place, including sales performance.
   - project work;
   - contribution to various practices, including networking;
   - contribution to various sectors, including networking;
   - collegiate contribution, including support to teams and colleagues;
   - personal development.
2. A number of hard targets are agreed and reviewed throughout the year. These will include sales and billings. In addition they may include:
   - increased involvement within a sector or practice;
   - taking the lead on specific projects or with certain clients;
   - achieving better relationships or increased sales with a specific client;
   - practice development.
3. The personal performance plan will map not just *what* has to be achieved but *how* the targets are to be achieved. In addition to specific measures of performance, the consultant is able to judge himself/herself against specific competencies. These competencies define the actions and behaviours which lead to superior performance. Table 11.3 shows an extract from a consultant's personal performance plan.
4. Once the performance plan has been agreed with the regional operations director, the consultant is expected to *make it happen* by soliciting input from a variety of sources, maximising opportunities, reviewing own performance and defining any development needs.
5. The performance review is carried out twice a year between the consultant and regional operations director. It is a joint review of performance achieved against the targets in the personal performance plan, drawing on the following information:
   - feedback and evidence from colleagues and clients;
   - the consultant's views;
   - the regional operations director's views.
6. At the end of each performance review meeting, the consultant and the regional operations director will have:

- a clear understanding of how the consultant has performed since the last review meeting;
- an agreed personal performance plan for the next period;
- agreed development actions.

7. Performance is rated on a scale A to E with clear reasons given for the rating. The rating is one of the factors used to determine the pay review for the consultant. The others are:
   - the pay review budget;
   - how much the consultant is already paid.

By taking a total approach to performance management the company is able to identify those factors which produce exceptional performers and it has the means to differentiate between the best and the rest, through the reward and succession planning policies.

The reward policy has so far emphasised *individual* achievement; let us now look at the team contribution.

Individual vs team performance

Recently the company introduced multi-practice teams into the organisation. Each consultant is placed into a team (of about 10 people) and the team is expected to be an operational unit, with agreed sales targets. Consultants also contribute to others' teams within the company. This development has raised the interesting issue of the potential tension between individual and team contributions.

Currently the reward arrangements reflect mainly individual contributions on sales and billings targets. There is a consideration of 'collegiate contribution' but this is relatively lightly weighted compared with the individual performance against the 'hard' targets. The reward arrangements encourage behaviours which emphasise an *individual* contribution rather than team orientation.

The teams are expected to be largely self-managing. So in order to reinforce this organisational unit it is revising its reward arrangements in order to put more emphasis on individual contributions to the team and overall team performance. In the future, team contribution will have a heavier weighting in the reward package; individuals and teams will be rewarded according to how well they have done against their agreed targets.

SUMMARY

The principle of self-management is one of the cornerstones of effective performance management. As more and more organisations move towards empowered structures and processes with a greater emphasis on self-managed individuals/teams, it will become critical to make sure that the performance management process reflects this development and that the reward arrangements reinforce the behaviours required to make 'self-management' a reality.

Self-management and development is not easy – it requires structure and support systems. The organisation cannot abdicate its overall responsibility for ensuring that all its people are focused on the right vision, values, goals and priorities, and that they are enabled to achieve these.

Ultimately, it is a question of getting the right balance between the organisation, the team and the individual.

References

1. *Economist* (1994) 19 March 1994; 'Managing People – nicely does it' (page 94) UK
2. Cook, S and Macauley, S (1993) 'Efficiency through self-appraisal' *Managing Service Quality*, November.
3. Buchanan, D (1987) 'Job enrichment is dead; long live high performance work designs' *Personnel Management*, May 1987, UK
4. Townsend, P and Gebhardt, J (1990) 'Quality – down to the roots' *Journal for Quality and Participation*, September 1990, UK.
5. Hoerr, J (1989) 'The Pay-off from Teamwork' *Business Week UK,* 10 July 1990
6. Bechard, R (1972) 'Optimising Team Building Efforts' *Journal of Contemporary Business*, USA, volume 1 (3), pp. 23–32

Chapter 12

Effective Links With Rewards

TODAY'S DILEMMAS

Linking pay to performance is viewed as a critical factor in business success by most organisations. How the two are linked is determined by their strategy, organisation design, culture, climate and perhaps the prevailing 'dogma' of the time. In these days of flatter organisations, increased customer and quality focus, and greater empowerment, the link between pay and performance is being re-examined and, in many cases, redefined. Yet in many employee attitude surveys, employees think that there are poor links between their performance management process and the reward system – in other words they do not see a real, credible link between what they and others have contributed and what they and others get paid. In these situations – and there is evidence to suggest that it is a widespread feeling – there is very little motivational value gained from linking performance and pay.

In previous chapters we have emphasised the importance of ensuring that the reward system is aligned to other human resource management processes, including performance management. A well designed and implemented reward system should reward the 'right' kind of results and the 'right' kind of behaviours, i.e. those which reinforce and enhance what the company is trying to achieve. Also a reward system which incorporates non-pay elements will go further towards motivating all employees than a strictly 'cash only' reward policy.

Employees are reconsidering their position on this issue by asking three questions:

1. Should pay for performance be delivered as *base salary* or a periodic *incentive*?
2. Should pay for performance be based on *individual* or *team* results or a *combination* of both?
3. Should pay for performance be focused on the *job* or the *person* performing the job?

THE RANGE OF APPROACHES

- ❑ The most traditional (and still most common) approach is the *merit increase*. The focus here is on base salary and rewarding the individual achievement of job results. The pay delivery vehicle is a job-specific salary range that is wide enough to accommodate all levels of performance (from 'needs improvement' to 'exceeds expectations') and a merit increase matrix that considers both performance level and position in salary range.
- ❑ A more progressive approach in recent years has been the combination of the individual merit increase with *a periodic* (usually annual) *incentive* that is based on individual and/or team results. This has been a successful way of introducing a variable (performance-related) component into what has traditionally been a totally fixed cost of doing business, thus sharing some risk with the employee.
- ❑ The current debate in pay for performance centres around the question of *rewarding job results vs job holder competencies* – in other words should we pay for what has been achieved or what the person is capable of achieving or both? This changes the

focus of pay for performance from being entirely retrospective to having a strong prospective component – in this approach pay is used to reinforce acquisition of skills and demonstration of competencies, as well as the performance of currently-assigned work. The pay delivery vehicle that has emerged to house this approach is *broad banding,* where the salary range is broadened to cover multiple levels of work

THE RATIONALE FOR PERFORMANCE-RELATED PAY

These different approaches to pay presuppose that pay motivates employees to perform better in their jobs. All organisations are engaged in a search for increased added-value from their employees and many see pay for performance as a critical element in achieving that goal. The assumption is made that employees have the power to control the amount of effort they put into the job and that they adjust their effort solely or mainly in relation to the monetary return they get from it.

Experience in designing and implementing all types of salary administration programmes has shown that there is a *threshold* in the amount of salary increase/bonus that must be available to influence an employee's job performance. Research conducted by Lawler[1] in the United States indicates that a pay increase of 3–4 per cent, while noticeable, is not sufficient to improve performance. He suggests that a pay rise of 10–15 per cent is probably required to increase motivation significantly.

Thus, in times when organisations' ability to give extra pay is noticeably limited, attempts to grant true 'pay for performance' may be suspended in favour of a general increase to all or most employees – and clearly communicated as such. At a time of low inflation, employers may take the view that they should not be contributing to pay drift and that there is no obligation to do more than maintain the purchasing power of competent performers, although presumably if they believe in performance-related pay at all, they must be prepared to provide higher rewards to outstanding performers.

What is perhaps one of the most powerful arguments for performance pay is that it is right and proper for people to be rewarded in accordance with their contribution. It is more equitable to differentiate rewards between employees performing at different levels in the same job.

This principle is summarised successfully in a recent draft report on the introduction of PRP in the Civil Service – 'The motivation was to reflect a new perception of equity based on the view that it is fairer to reward in relation to personal contribution rather than to reward for length of service in a particular post'.

On the other hand, experience has also shown that proven practice of distributing available salary/bonus money to all employees based on credible performance results can be a positive influence on employee performance. In this case, getting a 'better than average' increase, even if it is modest, can be motivating.

The amount of performance-related pay available will depend on the type of organisation, its culture and what it is prepared and able to pay. A performance-oriented, high-achieving organisation will offer high rewards in line with its high expectations consistent with what it can afford. If the organisation wants to retain good quality, high performing employees whose skills are much in demand it will have to take account of the market rates of progression for those people. A meaningful increase in one organisation for a particular individual may be significantly higher or lower than what other organisations would be prepared to pay. One organisation may feel that it has to pay its top performers 20–30 per cent above market median, while another would be content with 8–10 per cent or even less – much less in parts of the public sector.

PERFORMANCE-RELATED PAY – THE PARADOX

Performance-related pay in the United Kingdom is proving to be a puzzle. There is overwhelming scepticism about its effects on performance, yet its progress seems unstoppable. A study in 1991 by the National Economic Development Office found that about half of all private sector organisations in Britain were using performance-related pay for some staff and more than one-third had been doing so for more than ten years. Over the past five years pay systems linking base salaries to performance have spread rapidly in private industry and more recently in the public sector. The number of employees in Britain covered by some type of performance-related scheme is approaching 5 million, one-fifth of the British workforce.

The most recent research from the Institute of Manpower Studies reveals that more than two-thirds of all UK organisations now have individual-based performance-related pay for at least some of their staff. The majority of schemes apply to managers or valued 'core' staff but the trend of the past few years has been for the system to trickle down to all white collar staff. There has been widespread use of productivity-based bonus schemes for blue collar workers for many years.

While little work has been done to evaluate systematically the effectiveness of performance-related pay schemes, in recent months several reports have cast doubts on their motivational value for the majority of employees and have implied that they are not working, particularly in the public sector. The report of the Institute of Manpower Studies[2] examined the attitudes of nearly 1000 employees in three organisations operating individual-based performance-related pay schemes (a County Council, a food retailer, a building society).

The results of the analysis clearly show that in these three organisations the benefits most often claimed for performance-related pay were not met in practice. Firstly, it did not motivate (even those with high performance ratings). Secondly, there was little evidence to suggest that it helped to retain high performers and no evidence that poor performers left the organisations. Thirdly, employees were negative or broadly neutral on its impact on 'changing the culture'. Finally, employees were unclear as to whether the performance-related pay schemes were rewarded on a fair basis.

A similar review in the Inland Revenue (for 68,000 staff) claims that the scheme is regarded by employees as demotivating.[3] The inquiry found that staff morale about the scheme was at rock bottom. Among the complaints were that managers were regularly shifting targets upwards – effectively moving the goal posts; that pay differentials were insufficient to offer any incentive; and that many appraisals were conducted by managers who did not know the staff concerned. It was also alleged that senior managers were 'feathering their own nests' at the expense of more junior colleagues.

Staff complained that targets had been imposed on them by managers rather than reached by agreement, which was the stated aim. Difficulty was encountered in defining 'quality of work', in assessing staff, and employees at all grades were unhappy with the criteria based on subjective judgements. Some staff felt that the establishment of individual targets worked against attempts to foster a more cooperative work environment.

These criticisms reflect the views of Kohn[4] who argues that if employees lack enthusiasm for their job, financial rewards are ineffective at motivating people and that the more complicated the job, the less valid is the system that links pay to performance. He also argues that rewards discourage note-taking and make employees less imaginative and warns that the negative side of the system is that employees who go unrewarded feel they are being punished and their performance suffers.

On the other hand, the report of the Civil Service Review Body on senior salaries[5] concludes that the principle of relating pay to performance is substantially accepted by senior civil servants. Many of them now believe that they can influence their pay by how they perform.

THE LESSONS FROM EXPERIENCE

These reviews of the effectiveness of performance-related pay schemes strengthen the belief that performance-related pay cannot work effectively without a strong performance management process. Line managers and other employees should be able to define clearly 'what success looks like' for the organisation, the department and individuals and jointly set realistic targets and assess how well they have been achieved. When this performance management process is working well – and it usually takes two to three years to get bedded down – the organisation should consider linking performance to the pay system if it considers that it is appropriate to its strategy, culture and values. An integrated approach to performance management (without the pay link) can motivate all employees by providing a more satisfying and empowered work climate.

The reviews indicate the importance of taking a broader view of 'reward' other than just extra pay. The power of non-financial recognition as a motivator is often overlooked and undervalued. An effectively implemented 'recognition' scheme can reinforce a performance-based distribution of pay. In those organisations which eschew performance-related pay approaches, particularly in the public service, non-pay recognition becomes the sole means of motivating the good performers.

Recognition can be relatively informal – a culture that emphasises public praise for a job well done – or considerably more formal – with an established programme that rewards planned or spontaneous performance with merchandise or like awards. For example, in a Hospital Trust in the UK, the rewards for good performance have been widened to include additional days of leave, extra study facilities, 'employee of the month' awards (dinner for two...). Their reward strategy document sums it up neatly: 'if the pay is right, but non-pay is wrong, the reward strategy will fail'. The key to success is in the consistency with which it is implemented and with which it reinforces other forms of rewarding performance.

Behavioural reinforcement is the initial process of recognising and praising behaviour. It is a powerful motivational technique for shaping, rewarding and encouraging the recurrence of certain behaviours. Reinforcement should:

❑ identify *both* what the employee did effectively and *why* it is

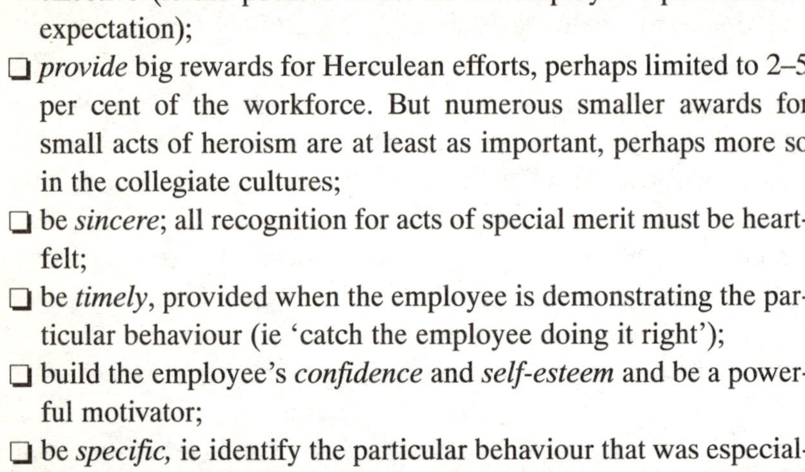

effective (ie the positive effect on the employee's performance expectation);

- *provide* big rewards for Herculean efforts, perhaps limited to 2–5 per cent of the workforce. But numerous smaller awards for small acts of heroism are at least as important, perhaps more so in the collegiate cultures;
- be *sincere*; all recognition for acts of special merit must be heartfelt;
- be *timely*, provided when the employee is demonstrating the particular behaviour (ie 'catch the employee doing it right');
- build the employee's *confidence* and *self-esteem* and be a powerful motivator;
- be *specific,* ie identify the particular behaviour that was especially effective. Celebrate what you want to see more of;
- identify both the *results* and the *competencies* demonstrated in achieving those end results. By reinforcing the behaviours that led to the results, it supports the continued demonstration of these behaviours.

There are some limitations to the way in which recognition systems can be operated in the public sector. But these limitations are often exaggerated as an excuse for not developing recognition options for employees. In public sector organisations recognition is likely to be more appropriate to the work cultures and effective as a motivator, than just performance-related pay. For example: a note from the chairman, a letter from the chief executive, a hand-written note from all of the top team in a department can be as effective as cash awards; halls of fame within a department (changing monthly); recognition events with small personal gifts are all possible. It is the fact of recognition and the sincerity of the act of recognition that count more than the monetary value of such actions.

MANAGING WORK CLIMATE THROUGH REWARDING PERFORMANCE

If performance-related pay is based upon an integrated performance management process, then it too could have a beneficial impact on the work climate. The climate dimensions which were described in Chapter 10 will be affected by the manner in which performance is rewarded, for example:

- *Clarity*: Employees need to recognise the link between performance expectations and rewards. A clear linkage should be made as early as the performance planning discussion. Employees can then recognise and appreciate what they would receive for meeting different performance levels.

  Whatever tangible and/or intangible rewards are provided, managers should explain to employees why the reward is offered, otherwise employees may feel that the reward was arbitrary. By reinforcing and rewarding specific behaviours and letting employees know what those behaviours are, employees are likely to perform them again in the future.
- ***Standards***: Employees need to realise that the standard for which they are striving is meeting their expectations, and that performing at this level will be tied to receiving certain rewards. As employees come to realise that meeting their own performance objectives is linked with meeting organisational objectives they will appreciate that rewards are provided when organisational objectives are met.

  Since an employee's goal is to meet his or her expectations, managers should guard against inadvertently implying that acceptable performance is less valuable than performance which exceeds expectations. Managers need to positively reinforce how the employee earned the reward at whatever level of actual performance is achieved. Of course, rewards should not be offered if employees did *not* meet their standards and there were no major obstacles that prevented them from doing so. Giving rewards in these instances will break the perceived link between meeting standards and getting rewarded appropriately.

- ***Responsibility***: It is important for employees to feel that they have responsibility over the rewards they will receive. By tying rewards to performance expectations, and letting employees know that you are available to provide help and support so that they can reach and exceed their expectations, you will give employees responsibility for making the effort needed to pursue rewards.
- ***Rewards***: Many managers make the assumption that a reward that is valued by one employee will be valued by all employees. Actually there are individual differences in what employees desire and find motivating. In recognising these individual differences, managers should think about rewards more broadly than just pay-linked options. As indicated earlier, it is possible to provide positive acknowledgement of success through means other than compensation. Rewards can provide the incentive to work towards performance standards only when the rewards are valued.
- ***Flexibility***: Clarifying the link between rewards and performance should encourage high flexibility because employees are motivated to minimise unnecessary procedures and develop new ideas and approaches.
- ***Team commitment***: Clearly where rewards are focused on team performance and/or emphasise collegiate or corporate contribution then they are likely to encourage individuals to cooperate, share information and resources. Individuals will understand that their success does not come at the expenses of their colleagues, but, instead, everyone working together increases the success of each member of the team.

INTEGRATING COMPETENCIES, PERFORMANCE AND PAY

As more organisations turn to a 'mixed model' performance management process to complement their flatter and more flexible structures, they need to consider how to integrate competencies, performance and pay.

We looked at how organisations are changing in Chapter 3 and we identified the impact of these changes on how people will manage and be managed. The key features were:

- Work is being organised in a more flexible way.
- Individuals can no longer be valued merely by looking at the 'job' they do. In the delayered organisation there is scope for individuals to grow in *roles*.
- With fewer managers left in organisations, there has to be more focus on self-development and self-management. Competency language is increasingly being used to describe how people could improve their performance in their jobs, and what additional competencies are required to do bigger or different roles.
- Performance management is increasingly incorporating competencies ('mixed models').

The integration of these features is shown in Figure 12.1.

We have come to recognise that employees are not just units of output but are units of contribution. Contribution takes into account the impact on individual behaviours, skills and motives on individual performance, ie competencies.

Complete performance from individuals can only be managed if we recognise that it is not only *what* is done which is important but also *how* it is done. If this is the way we are going to manage individual performance in the future then reward systems, which are an integral part of performance management, must be capable of reflecting and reinforcing competencies.

THE PROBLEMS WITH REWARDING ASSOCIATED COMPETENCIES

This broader view of jobs has led many organisations to the point where they are integrating competencies in the reward arrangements for certain jobs. If jobs are regarded as units of contribution

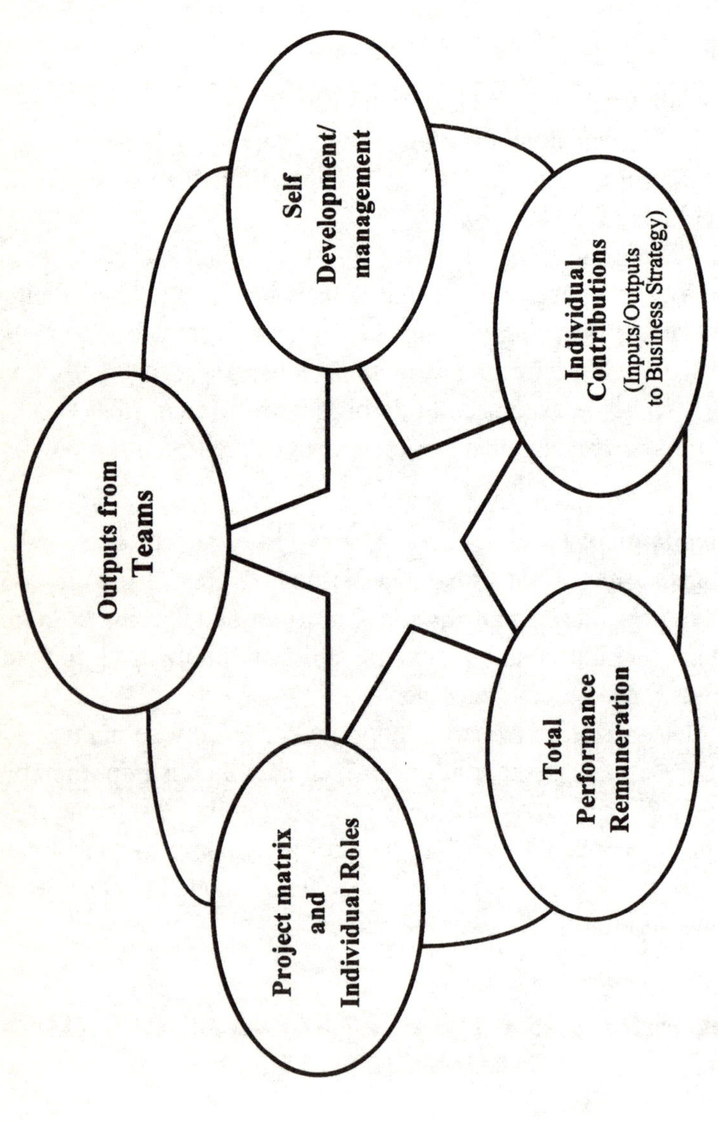

Figure 12.1 *How organisations are managed in the mid-1990s model*

and a driver of contribution is the competency profile required for superior performance, then we have to take account of competencies in the way people are rewarded.

However, we do have to be very careful in how pay and competencies are linked. There can be pitfalls associated with rewarding performance using competencies which, unless resolved, can negate the effectiveness of the whole approach. Linking competencies to pay runs the risk of incurring significant extra payroll costs without creating added value to the business. The main problems to be resolved are as follows.

They are input based

One potential problem with rewarding competencies is that they describe inputs to jobs. The link to outputs is based on a validation that possession of those competencies results in improved performance. Competency profiling and assessment techniques can help us to identify those competencies which predict superior performance, but they are still inputs. Merely possessing them does not translate automatically to superior performance unless the job holder makes good use of them through effective performance management processes.

Paying for inputs can be a costly exercise unless we are sure that they are translated into desired outputs. People will acquire new skills and competencies merely to earn the additional pay, they will migrate to the top of pay scales and remuneration costs will drift upwards unless suitable controls are put into place.

We have to get the right balance between paying for the achievement of objectives and the possession of competencies.

We need pay systems which recognise the importance of competencies in individual performance but provide the kind of controls and checks which avoid pay drift and paying solely for input.

Is the competency model valid?

Another potential problem which can have significant implications for the payroll costs of the business is the validity of the competency models proposed.

If a business wishes to link individual pay in some form or other to a competency profile, there has to be a high degree of confidence that individuals who attain the desired levels in the competencies really are going to make a greater contribution to the business. If the follow-through into outputs is not evident and closely monitored, payroll costs will increase with little or no business advantage.

It is important, therefore, that the competency model proposed has high validity. This will impact upon the process used for devising the model. The competencies agreed upon must be proven to make a positive difference to performance. You must be convinced that possessing and demonstrating the competencies explains the difference between superior and average performance in any job.

Can they be properly measured?

There must also be robust measuring processes for assessing individual performance in competency language. Woolly definitions and imprecisely worded descriptions of competency levels will result in poor assessment of individual performance.

Examples of how competencies should be defined for assessment purposes are given in Chapter 8.

In order to ensure that we get value for money from competency based pay structures we have to do one of two things:

1. control the progression, and hence salary costs, of job holders; and
2. ensure that progression, where it occurs, translates into outputs by improved performance.

COMPETENCY-BASED PAY SYSTEMS

There are, broadly, two different approaches to recognising competencies in reward arrangements:

1. Incorporating them into 'merit' based pay schemes.
2. Building competency-based pay structures.

Merit based pay schemes

Many companies have a typical 'merit' based pay scheme where the outcome of an individual performance appraisal is used to drive the increase in base salary.

Some have worked on defining competency requirements and wish to take account of them within the existing pay scheme. In some cases this is for specific jobs where tailored competency profiles have been devised or it may be for several 'generic' competencies which they wish to develop in all employees in the business, irrespective of the job they are doing.

The way in which these companies have chosen to reflect competencies in reward is to incorporate them into the performance management process. The required competency profile is included in the stated performance requirements for the job and the individual's actual performance in comparison with the requirements (including competencies) is taken into account when awarding an overall performance rating. This approach may be a suitable way of introducing competencies into existing reward arrangements. The nature of the pay linkage through the appraisal process will be familiar to people and the effect of the additional competency element will be contained within the framework of the overall performance rating. This approach also controls the acquisition of competencies by job holders. It ensures that job holders' progression is consistent not only with the capabilities of the person, but also in accordance with the needs of the business.

Competency-based pay structures

The traditional approach of defining a job role (and hence its size and reward) using accountabilities and/or responsibilities needs to be supplemented for some jobs. The accountabilities may span a number of different levels at which the job may be performed.

These kind of jobs are usually knowledge jobs and are often referred to as 'job families' or 'job ladder'. They include professional ladders such as scientists, engineers, accountant etc as well as clerical or administrative roles. The different levels on the ladder may well have the same set of accountabilities or responsibilities. Ladders have existed for some time and have usually been defined in terms of the additional levels of knowledge or experience which are necessary to move from one level to another.

The use of competencies has opened up the possibility of bringing other kinds of jobs into ladder structures, notably customer service jobs where behaviours and skills can drive job performance. The factor which differentiates between the levels in a competency-based model is the acquisition of or development of competencies.

There are two particular aspects which generally characterise ladder jobs. Firstly, movement between the levels on these ladders is totally dependent upon the job holder acquiring the necessary competencies and does not depend upon the availability of a vacancy. As a result, job holders progress from one level to the other over time as soon as they have demonstrated the necessary competencies. It is therefore possible for a team of people to start off at the lowest ladder level and steadily progress up the 'rungs' until they are all at the highest level.

Secondly, there is usually an upper limit to ladder progression. At some point, the exact nature of which is dependent upon the job, further progression is dependent upon 'promotion' which is not necessarily competency-based and needs a vacancy.

In pay terms, the different levels on the ladder usually carry different levels of remuneration to reflect the increasing level of performance which is expected from job holders at higher levels.

This kind of structure, of course, has potentially significant implications for competency-based reward. If each ladder level has different remuneration arrangements, progression up the ladder automatically means an increase in the level of pay. There is a real risk of paying for input only.

The problem is minimised again by a judicious choice of criteria for defining the competencies. The competency model must be:

- based upon competencies which really do drive *superior* performance. In this way, acquiring those competencies will almost certainly translate into higher contribution and justify the higher level of remuneration;
- clear about the requirements for moving to different levels so that there is a real improvement in performance;
- based upon the competencies that reflect the real needs of the organisation.

The kind of competency-based pay structure which could apply to 'ladder' jobs is shown in Figure 12.2. This structure embraces competency acquisition, competency demonstration and performance against agreed standards at the different levels.

Competency-based pay – getting the right fit

Generally speaking competency-based pay will be appropriate where an organisation wishes to highlight and reward certain behaviours and skills (which it believes will lead to improved performance).

Spencer and Spencer[6] have listed those organisational conditions which may indicate the need for a competency-based pay approach:

- inability of the organisation to attract 'good' (ie more competent than average) employees;
- the perception that people with certain competencies add more value to the firm than those without them in identical jobs;
- the perception that job-based pay systems are inappropriate when change is so fast that the very concept of a (stable) 'job' may have lost meaning. In these situations, a person either has many 'jobs' or roles or the 'person makes the job'; the value added to

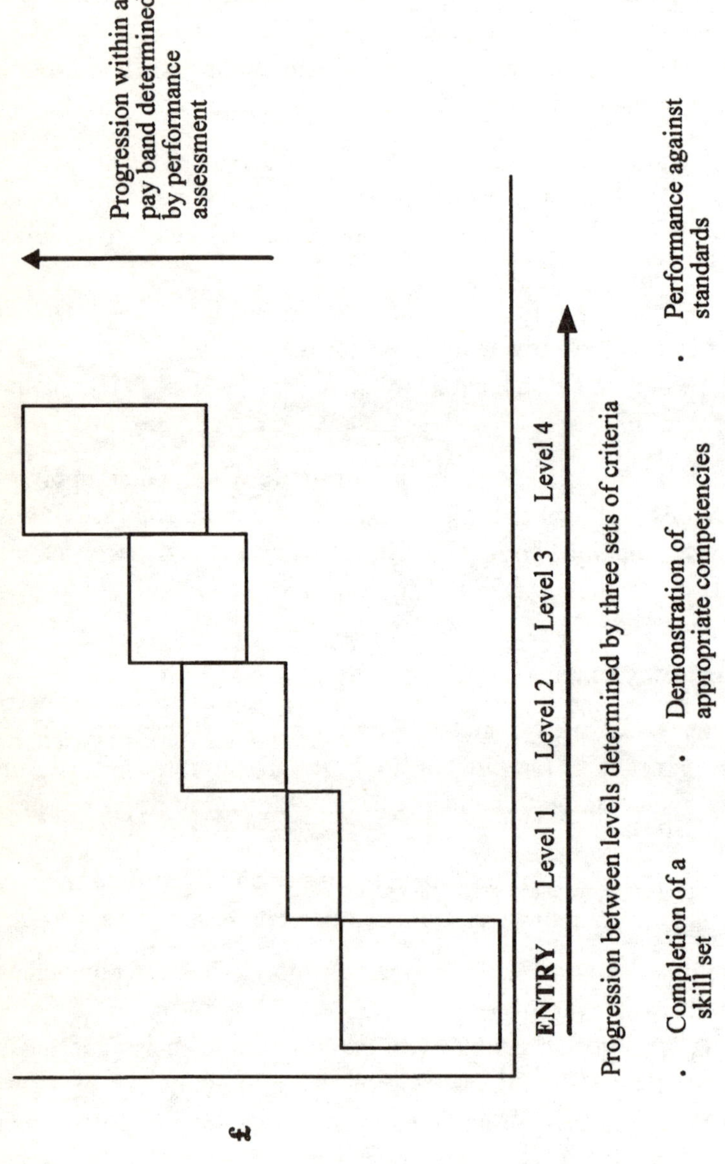

Figure 12.2 *Linking competency and performance-related pay*

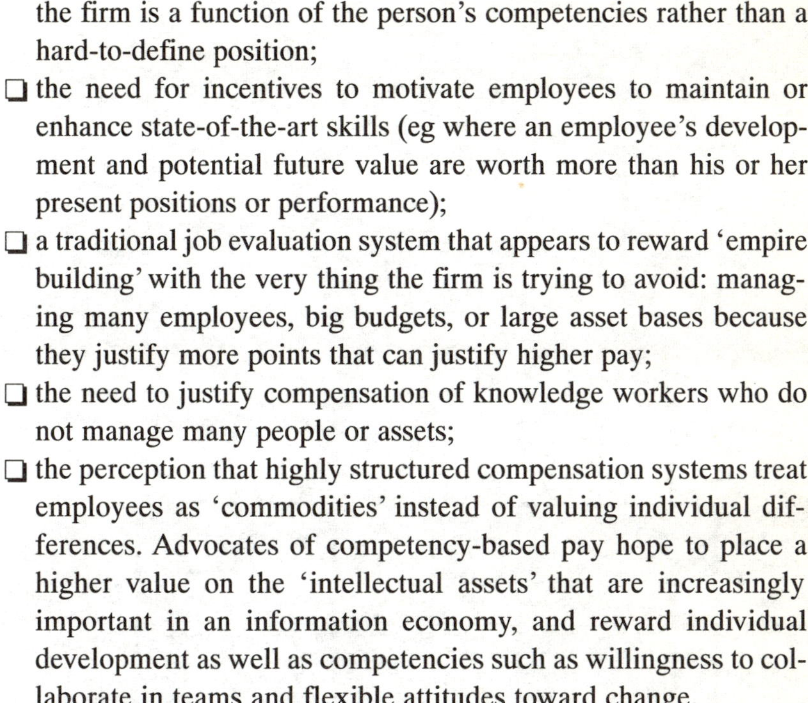

the firm is a function of the person's competencies rather than a hard-to-define position;

- the need for incentives to motivate employees to maintain or enhance state-of-the-art skills (eg where an employee's development and potential future value are worth more than his or her present positions or performance);
- a traditional job evaluation system that appears to reward 'empire building' with the very thing the firm is trying to avoid: managing many employees, big budgets, or large asset bases because they justify more points that can justify higher pay;
- the need to justify compensation of knowledge workers who do not manage many people or assets;
- the perception that highly structured compensation systems treat employees as 'commodities' instead of valuing individual differences. Advocates of competency-based pay hope to place a higher value on the 'intellectual assets' that are increasingly important in an information economy, and reward individual development as well as competencies such as willingness to collaborate in teams and flexible attitudes toward change.

A balanced total performance reward approach

Competency-based pay is clearly an approach which will benefit many organisations but it is risky if it neglects the output side of the question. For some employees output based pay is a real incentive (despite the criticisms outlined earlier) and bonus schemes do have a positive impact in empowering individual or team focus on specific results.

Therefore most organisations adopting the competency-based pay route are also seeking to link pay with outputs. Increasingly this is being done through use of bonuses – and these are becoming more clearly directed to be part of an effective remuneration package.

Putting together the package is the key. A total performance reward approach uses a range of individual, team and organisational performance rewards (and includes competencies in the 'performance

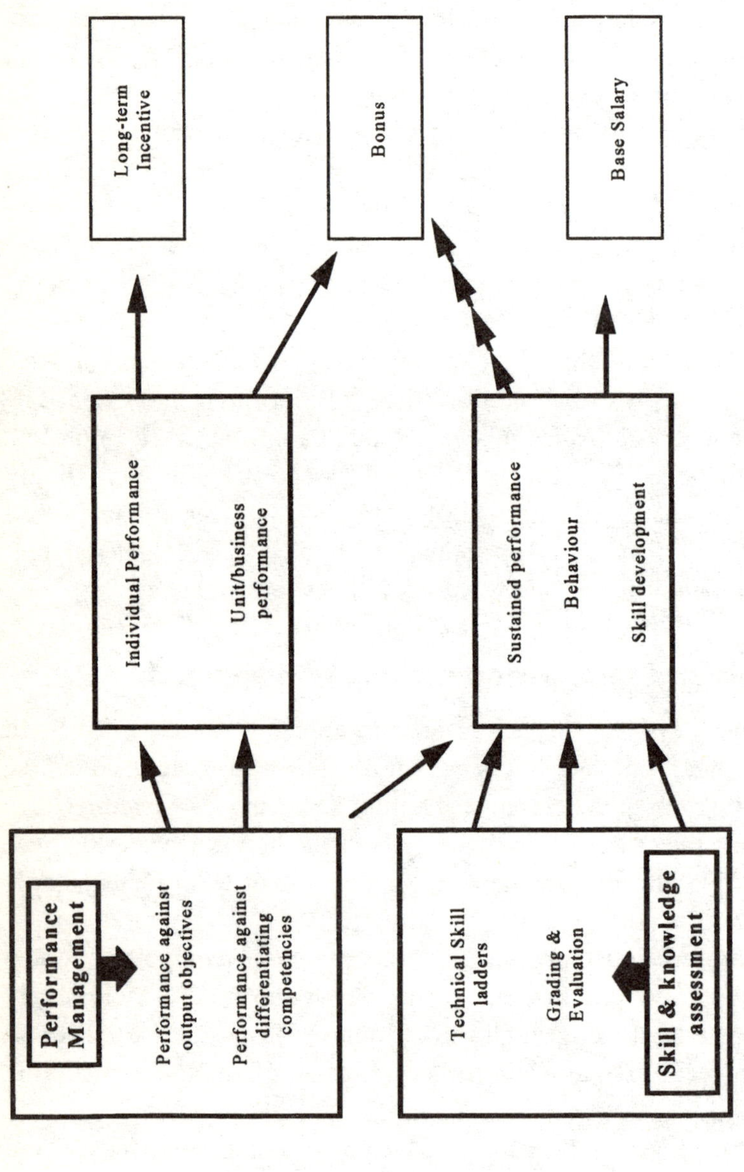

Figure 12.3 *A possible model for rewards linked to performance*

equation'). This recognises the different facets and layers of performance and emphasises the messages that can be delivered through reward management processes to reinforce success.

Figure 12.3 illustrates the total performance reward package being use by a large UK-based energy company.

SUMMARY

We know from the experience in many organisations that linking performance and pay is not a panacea for performance improvement. This linkage creates its own set of problems and unless it is carefully designed and managed, it can have a damaging effect on the performance management process and on other aspects of organisational life. But many organisations believe that it is the right approach for them – they do wish to reward the better performers with better rewards (than average/competent performers).

Whichever approach is chosen by the organisation it should reinforce the organisation's objectives and fit its work culture(s). Furthermore if a competency-based approach to performance management is in place (or being developed) the organisation has to decide how to link competencies, performance and pay.

The final point to emphasise is that 'rewards' go beyond pay. All individuals need to feel valued and recognised by the organisation for the work they deliver. Organisations have got to develop more creative approaches for rewarding individuals/teams than they have used in the past.

References

1. Lawler, E (1988) 'Pay for Performance, Making it work' *Personnel,* October, UK
2. Thompson, M (1993) *Pay and Performance – The Employee Experience* Institute of Manpower Studies, Report 258
3. Deacon, M (1994) *An Inquiry into Performance-Related Pay in the Inland Revenue* HMSO, UK
4. Kohn, A (1994) 'Why Incentive Plans Cannot Work' *Harvard*

Business Review, September, USA

5. Review Body on Senior Salaries (1994): *Report No 34* HMSO, February
6. Spencer, L and Spencer, S (1993) *Competence at Work* Wiley, USA

Chapter 13

Making it Happen – An Action Plan

WHERE TO START?

We have been on a long journey to re-engineer the performance management process. We have identified the seven key components of an effective performance management process, ie one which is capable of reinforcing and supporting major change initiatives in your organisation.

You might not have all of these elements in place. Or you might decide that you do not want to embrace all of them. So you need to decide where to start and how to close the gaps between your current arrangements and your 'ideal' model. It might be useful to use the Model of Change and Improvement which was described in Chapter 11 (see Figure 13.1) This six-step model will give you a systematic framework for deciding what to do and how to assess success. Then you have to work out how you are going to implement your ideas.

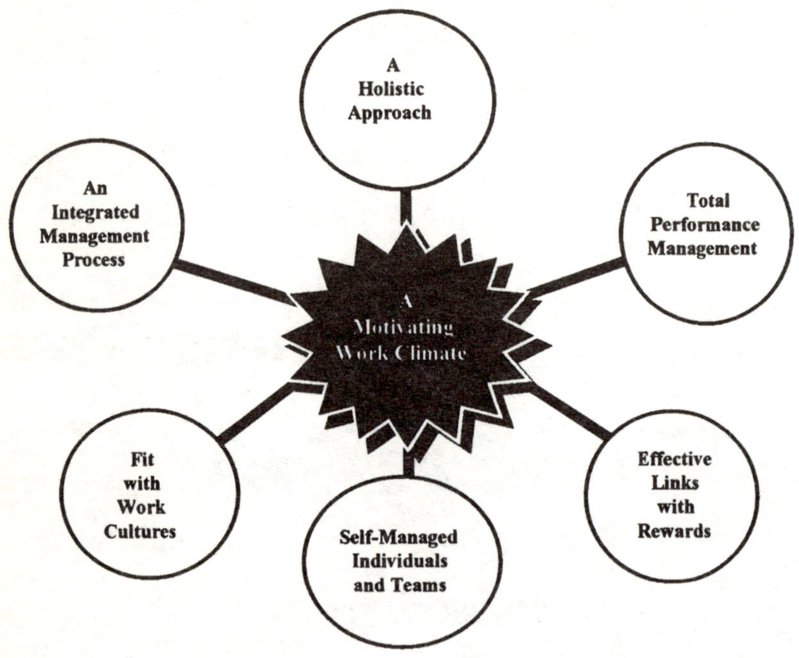

IMPLEMENTING PERFORMANCE MANAGEMENT – THE CRITICAL SUCCESS FACTORS

Successful performance management stems from a combination of a demonstrable commitment from the senior managers and from investment (of time and resources) into developing and training people to deliver good performance. Designing a performance management process is the easier part; introducing it and making it work is much more difficult. We know that the majority of performance management processes fail to make their mark on their organisations and this is chiefly due to how the processes are implemented. So how do you implement?

Here are some critical success factors:

- ❑ ***Performance management should be 'owned' by all staff***: In those organisations where procedures and paperwork dominate the performance management process it is likely to be regarded

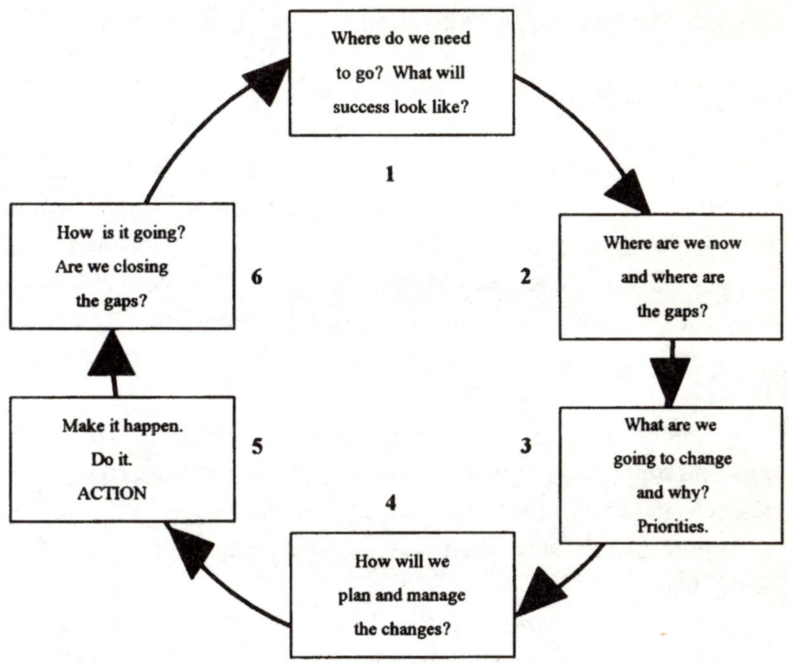

Figure 13.1 *A model for change and improvement*

by employees as an administrative burden and a needless irritation. Emotionally 'it does not belong to them'.

This sense of ownership is developed by involving staff in all stages of the introduction of the process, including design, implementation and audit.

- ***The performance management process should not be driven by 'pay'***: The performance management process has a value with or without a pay link. It needs to be positioned as an important management process in its own right. Research into employee motivation indicates that there is a wide range of factors which motivate performance. Evidence from employee attitude surveys points to money taking third or fourth place behind such factors as job satisfaction, job challenge, recognition, attractive career opportunities, training and development, a good work climate, supportive management styles and pleasant working conditions. Long-term, sustainable motivation is rarely money driven.

The focus now is on looking for what motivates people of different kinds in the organisation. Money is one of the many motivators; it rarely drives performance on its own. Performance-related pay can be part of the performance contract. In isolation it does not deliver performance improvement because it is not usually the primary motivator for increased effort. We have seen (in Chapter 9) that in some organisations individual performance-related pay can be detrimental in certain work cultures and structures, eg team-based, collegiate organisations.

- ***Senior managers should set and communicate an overall strategy and key strategic goals***: A strategic plan enables senior managers to guide and focus the effort of all employees in a common direction and to show their own commitment to managing performance.

  Performance management is the process which organisations should use to link these corporate targets with individual/team contributions, through the setting of measurable objectives. By setting clear objectives for teams and individuals everyone can see how they fit in to the organisation and what they need to do on a daily basis.
- ***Active support from top management***: This is vital and it must go beyond a formal go-ahead or a few words on the front of the performance management brochure. The best support is the top managers using the performance management process themselves with their staff and showing a genuine commitment to it.
- ***Running a 'pilot'/staged approach***: Sometimes it might be more sensible to run a pilot of the process in a part of the organisation, rather than go for the 'big bang' approach. In choosing the area for the pilot approach look for champions, not necessarily the areas where performance management may be easiest.

  Also it might be necessary to have a staged approach in order to gain support for the process. For example, you might prefer to try the processes out at one level or for one group, before extending it to others. A staged approach often builds support for performance management from the bottom up. A 'big bang' adds to the difficulties but may give the initiative a higher profile and achieve faster cultural change.

- ***Training for all in the key phases of performance management***: Effective performance management requires all staff to be skilled in the setting of objectives, monitoring and tracking of performance and the assessment of performance. It requires managers to create the kind of workplace climate which motivates their employees and encourages them to stretch their performance.

  Many organisations have underestimated the amount of training required to cover the full performance management cycle. It is likely to be at least three one-day workshops, which is more effective when it is spread across a 12 month performance management cycle.

  The focus of the training workshops should be to win hearts and minds of the staff. In other words they have to be a combination of skills training and developing positive attitudes to performance management, ie how to build trust, how to involve, create pride and a sense of openness to achieve consent and commitment at all levels, so that employees get the chance to make the best of themselves and make a special contribution to the organisation. The cold logic of the strategic plan must be translated into an inspiring vision, into a mission statement that the workforce can identify with and be proud of. This must be reinforced by a set of values which are recognised and understood by all employees. Ownership and commitment are nurtured through these workshops but they have to address the concerns and anxieties of the staff and be tailored to their particular needs.

  Some organisations phase the training programme so that everyone is trained in performance planning before the planning phase, followed by training in managing performance some months later, with training in reviewing performance just before the formal reviews take place at the end of the year.

  There should be on-going coaching and support after the initial implementation phase to ensure that the process maintains momentum. Obviously newly recruited staff should receive training when they join the organisation.

- ❑ ***Regard it as a 'learning process'***: You won't get it perfectly right in the first year or two. It is likely to take 3 – 4 years before it becomes reasonably well bedded down. 'Sticking with it' is important, but be flexible and brave enough to recognise the need for revision and improvement. Do not insist on perfection from the first day. You can give a powerful signal about the development of a performance–improvement culture by putting 'L' plates on the first years of implementation with a commitment to review and adapt.

  Once the process is installed, with start-up training for all participants, it is important to establish a framework for the monitoring of the effectiveness of the process. Evolution, revision and change will be necessary to achieve continuous improvement. To keep performance management moving forward you must first know how it is succeeding, or taking, to meet the objectives set:
  - what's working well?
  - what is not working well?
  - how could the process/application be improved?

  Common ways to monitor performance management are:

  - recording and analysing performance assessment. This helps establish how managers are using performance management;
  - sampling performance review documentation. This is a good indication of the nature of performance reviews;
  - one-to-one interviews with managers/staff to identify how they are finding the experience of performance management and where they need more support;
  - employee attitude surveys and/or focus discussion groups;
  - repeating the organisational surveys that you might have used before the process was introduced to the organisation, eg diagnostic questionnaire, organisational climate survey, management style questionnaires. This will enable you to assess the impact of the performance management process.

It is important for the long-term development of the process to identify areas of good practice and to disseminate it around the organisation. Make some 'Golden' awards to highlight the good role models around. In addition, to maintain high standards the following actions are useful:

- ❑ maintaining training in performance management for all new staff (including individuals who are promoted to management posts);
- ❑ top-up training to keep the principles and practices fresh;
- ❑ one-to-one coaching of managers;
- ❑ workshops for managers to share experiences.

It would be a very useful step to establish a taskforce/steering group to monitor the performance management process. This group should be representative of all staff and empowered to review and revise the process in the light of their analysis. This approach would reinforce the principle of getting staff to 'own' the process and to accept responsibility for its success.

Performance management processes can remain unchanged for several years, but with the high rate of change in organisations, it will probably need to develop, introduce new ideas and take on new objectives. In particular, when individuals/teams have mastered some practices in performance management, they may wish to take things forward themselves. In other words, to become more self-managed. They should be encouraged to do so. Normally, organisations undertake reviews of performance management every 3–5 years.

Managing expectations

In any change process there should be regular communications with staff to explain the purpose of change and how it will affect them. Unfortunately it is usually done too infrequently and/or too poorly. Employees are mainly interested in 'what it means to me' and want to be told what is happening and why. It needs to be told in good time. The communications initiative should be trying to capture 'hearts and minds'. Thus problems or potential problems need to be addressed and employees have a right to be heard as well as told. Without an effective, sustained communications strategy it is doubtful if you will be able to get employees to own the performance management process. Some organisations have set up special newsletters (usually called 'performance matters') to sustain staff interest and involvement.

All of these changes obviously involve careful training and preparation. The manner in which these changes are conducted is evolving too. In one major international pharmaceutical company, the head of management training reports:

> whenever we identify major projects involving change – in performance, in mentality, in knowledge and skills – we accompany these with change management programmes.
>
> We set up workshops and information projects before the implementation phase, involving the workers and asking for their opinion, and then we make detailed adjustments according to their suggestion.

Active involvement of this sort is essential, since the 'idea of changing the way that workers may work may be fine and easily explained on paper, but the actual implementation is much more profound and more delicate'. In one current change project, the company is devoting 10 per cent of the total cost of the project to educating and training the workforce.

Chapter 14

Summary

THE CONCEPT OF RE-ENGINEERING

The theme of this book is the re-engineering of the performance management process. We have looked at the seven steps which could lead to a step change in the performance management process. Business process re-engineering has as a foundation, in its original intent, focus on the customer. That is, all core business processes begin and end with satisfying the customer. Re-engineering is about reorientating the business processes from the perspective of the customer; of thinking in processes and not in functions and of ensuring that activities are adding value.

THE CUSTOMERS OF THE PERFORMANCE MANAGEMENT PROCESS

Clearly all members of staff are the 'real' customers of the performance management process. This is the client group for whom the process should be designed and operated. Very few organisations have bothered to find out what employees want from the process, but research carried out by Hay has identified that the most important needs of the performance management customers are:

- ❑ What am I expected to achieve in my job and how will success be judged?
- ❑ How am I doing?
- ❑ How are we doing? (relative to competitors)
- ❑ Where do I stand?
- ❑ Where am I going?
- ❑ What do I need to work on?

From the surveys described in Chapter 2 we know that the performance management process in many organisations is not satisfying internal customer needs. There is much work that has to be done to make them truly effective.

If the performance management process can satisfy its customer needs then it will be adding value to the organisation by enhancing employees' satisfaction and performance. Both employees and the organisation will gain from the process.

The rest of this chapter summarises the key themes set out in Part Two.

PERFORMANCE MANAGEMENT AS A CORE BUSINESS PROCESS

Effective performance management is the driving force in successful organisations which ensures that individuals and teams work together to achieve continued performance improvement. This means planning for performance improvement, coaching, managing progress continuously and recognising achievement. Performance management needs to be driven by top management and linked to the business planning process. It becomes the way in which strategic change is achieved, new cultures are built and business initiatives such as quality improvement and customer service are turned from ideas into reality. Managing total performance involves the creation of a working environment within which development, delivery and recognition of achievement happen on a continuous basis. Coaching and managing progress becomes everybody's job.

ALL ASPECTS OF PERFORMANCE MATTER

Many purely results-based approaches to performance management fail because they only capture the 'hard' elements of performance that can be targeted and measured. There are many jobs, particularly those whose prime objective is to improve customer service, where this approach is unlikely to work for them on its own. What matters more is *how* they go about their work, what competencies lead to superior performance and how these can be acquired, developed and improved. The performance management process must reflect a balance between measurable results and the demonstration of competencies which result in job-related success.

GETTING THE BEST FIT

It is important for every organisation to develop and refine its own approach to performance management. There is no perfect 'one model fits all' process. Each organisation (and indeed different parts of the organisation) needs to assess how performance should be managed and then design (with contributions from line managers and staff) a process to fit the environment. Then it needs to continually assess how well the process is serving the needs of its customers and of the organisation.

GETTING DISCRETIONARY EFFORT

Raising the level of performance is all about getting discretionary effort from employees. There is a need to ensure that there is an emphasis on progress and of continually pushing the boundaries of discretionary effort. We know that there are differentiating competencies that make the difference between good and superior performance. We know that there is, on average, a third difference between good and superior performance. Hay/McBer research has shown that by identifying these differentiating competencies and coaching for them the performance of employees will be enhanced.

But employees will only 'go the extra mile' if the workplace environment encourages and rewards them to do so. Hence the critical importance of developing managerial capability in the motivation of their staff by creating a positive workplace climate.

EFFECTIVE LINKS WITH REWARDS GET IMPORTANT MESSAGES ACROSS

Organisations dedicated to continuing performance improvement need to reflect this across their total approach to reward. Training, career development and non-financial personal and team recognition as rewards are at least as important as financial incentives and performance-related pay. Getting the balance right is critical. We know that pay systems on their own do not manage people or performance – and this is an important lesson from which many organisations have failed to learn. We also know that well-designed rewards – ie those which fit their particular work cultures of the organisation – will reinforce key business messages.

OWNERSHIP OF THE PROCESS IS KEY

Line managers and individuals need to believe in the way performance is managed so that they contribute the extra effort. Successful performance management harnesses both team and individual contribution rather than concentrating on one or the other. This means that defining and assessing performance is no longer just a management prerogative: It has to be an integral part of the managerial function. It is the day-to-day performance dialogue, the quality of discussion, the focus on development and providing recognition that are the real signs of a flourishing performance culture. All of these have to be line-management owned. The most effective and enduring performance management processes are developed with line managers and staff so that there is a proper 'fit' between the process and the 'real time' working practices.

Appendix 1

PERFORMANCE MANAGEMENT QUESTIONNAIRE
(For each phase of the PM cycle)

Scale: 1 = Strongly Disagree 2 = Disagree 3 = Hard to Decide 4 = Agree 5 = Strongly Agree

PERFORMANCE PLANNING

1.	Our organisation has clear business goals.	1	2	3	4	5
2.	My performance expectations are linked to the business plan.	1	2	3	4	5
3.	I am clear about the results I am expected to achieve in my job.	1	2	3	4	5
4.	I am clear about the behaviours that I am expected to demonstrate in my job.	1	2	3	4	5
5.	My supervisor and I see eye-to-eye on what my performance expectations are.	1	2	3	4	5
6.	My immediate supervisor and I worked together to plan my performance expectations.	1	2	3	4	5
7.	The results I am expected to achieve are:					
	❑ Specific	1	2	3	4	5
	❑ Measurable	1	2	3	4	5
	❑ Achievable	1	2	3	4	5
	❑ Relevant	1	2	3	4	5
	❑ Time-based	1	2	3	4	5
8.	I feel I have adequate involvement in establishing my performance expectations.	1	2	3	4	5
9.	My supervisor and I plan my performance expectations at the beginning of my new performance year.	1	2	3	4	5
10.	My supervisor has a good understanding of my job.	1	2	3	4	5

PERFORMANCE MANAGEMENT QUESTIONNAIRE

Scale: 1 = Strongly Disagree 2 = Disagree 3 = Hard to Decide 4 = Agree 5 = Strongly Agree

PERFORMANCE FEEDBACK & COACHING

1. My supervisor and I held Progress Reviews to discuss my performance in my job at least three times in the last year.	1	2	3	4	5
2. These discussions are effective in guiding my performance.	1	2	3	4	5
3. My immediate supervisor:	1	2	3	4	5
❑ Is easy to see or talk with when I have a work-related problem or need assistance in my job.	1	2	3	4	5
❑ Gives me the information or assistance I need to accomplish my performance expectations.	1	2	3	4	5
❑ Listens to what I have to say regarding my performance expectations.	1	2	3	4	5
❑ Encourages me when I need guidance or suggestions for accomplishing my performance expectations.	1	2	3	4	5
❑ Reinforces me when I am doing a good job.	1	2	3	4	5
❑ Lets me know when I am not meeting my performance expectations.	1	2	3	4	5
4. My supervisor gives me feedback on how I am doing towards achieving the results I am expected to accomplish.	1	2	3	4	5
5. My supervisor gives me feedback on how I am doing with regard to the behaviours I am expected to demonstrate on the job.	1	2	3	4	5

PERFORMANCE MANAGEMENT QUESTIONNAIRE

Scale: 1 = Strongly Disagree 2 = Disagree 3 = Hard to Decide 4 = Agree 5 = Strongly Agree

PERFORMANCE REVIEW

1.	Our organisation has a fair system for evaluating an employee's performance.	1	2	3	4	5
2.	I have a clear understanding of how my performance is judged.	1	2	3	4	5
3	My supervisor views my performance fairly.	1	2	3	4	5
4.	Poor performance is not tolerated in our organisation.	1	2	3	4	5
5.	There were no surprises in my most recent performance review because I was clear about what I was being evaluated on.	1	2	3	4	5
6.	I have a clear understanding of the rating scale used in the performance appraisal process.	1	2	3	4	5
7.	I know what I need to do to 'meet expectations' in my job.	1	2	3	4	5
8.	My most recent overall performance rating accurately reflected the results I have achieved.	1	2	3	4	5
9.	I am comfortable participating in discussions about my performance with my supervisor during my performance review.	1	2	3	4	5
10.	My performance reviews are conducted with me in a private setting.	1	2	3	4	5
11.	My supervisor and I worked together to design an individual development plan for me.	1	2	3	4	5
12.	My supervisor is able to effectively communicate the results of my performance in writing.	1	2	3	4	5
13.	I understand that I can provide my supervisor with information about my performance before my final performance review is written.	1	2	3	4	5
14.	The measures associated with the results I am expected to achieve accurately identify what is required of me in my job.	1	2	3	4	5

Appendix 2a

PERFORMANCE MANAGEMENT QUESTIONNAIRE

INSTRUCTIONS

For each of the following statements you must circle the number which best represents your current view.

It is important that you try to use the full range of responses and avoid neutral answers.

If you do not supervise staff, leave questions relating to 'your staff' and 'subordinates' blank.

My current view is

		strongly disagree		**neutral**		**strongly agree**
1.	There is a clear link with pay and performance.	1	2	3	4	5
2.	Training helps improve performance.	1	2	3	4	5
3.	Management really tackle poor performance.	1	2	3	4	5
4.	Individuals provide the highest quality of service.	1	2	3	4	5
5.	Appraisals are clearly linked to performance improvement.	1	2	3	4	5
6.	I know how to influence how I am rewarded.	1	2	3	4	5
7.	My role is clearly defined.	1	2	3	4	5
8.	Employees are offered challenging careers.	1	2	3	4	5
9.	I am free to use my own judgement.	1	2	3	4	5
10.	I know what the organisation's plans are.	1	2	3	4	5
11.	It is clear how my annual performance appraisal links to my pay.	1	2	3	4	5
12.	Quality is accepted as paramount in all that is done.	1	2	3	4	5
13.	Management try to avoid conflict during appraisals.	1	2	3	4	5
14.	I use the annual appraisal system to criticise my staff's performance.	1	2	3	4	5
15	Poor performance is clearly visible.	1	2	3	4	5
16.	The appraisal system helps me perform more effectively.	1	2	3	4	5

My current view is

	strongly disagree		neutral		strongly agree
17. There is openness and honesty in all that is done.	1	2	3	4	5
18. I know when my efforts have been recognised.	1	2	3	4	5
19. I am clear about my accountabilities.	1	2	3	4	5
20. I need more freedom in my job.	1	2	3	4	5
21. Enthusiasm and pride in work is the norm.	1	2	3	4	5
22. I know what the organisation's strategy is.	1	2	3	4	5
23. The current link between pay and performance is fair.	1	2	3	4	5
24. Monitoring standards of performance is a regular management activity.	1	2	3	4	5
25. Individual skills are pooled for collective success.	1	2	3	4	5
26. I am confident I will give recognition to my staff for good performance.	1	2	3	4	5
27. Poor performance is truly not tolerated.	1	2	3	4	5
28. I know when I am performing well in my job.	1	2	3	4	5
29. Promotion is clearly linked to performance.	1	2	3	4	5
30. I adequately explain to my staff how their pay is calculated.	1	2	3	4	5
31. All talents are used creatively.	1	2	3	4	5
32. My manager and I agree what my job responsibilities are.	1	2	3	4	5
33. I am able to exercise creativity in my job.	1	2	3	4	5
34. I am clear about how my role fits into the organisation's plan.	1	2	3	4	5
35. Employees are offered satisfying jobs.	1	2	3	4	5
36. My manager is able to use the current pay system to motivate me.	1	2	3	4	5
37. My staff are clear about my plans.	1	2	3	4	5
38. There is sufficient training and support given to staff.	1	2	3	4	5
39. I fully explain why decisions have to be made to my staff.	1	2	3	4	5

My current view is

	strongly disagree		neutral		strongly agree
40. My manager lets me know at the right time when my work is not acceptable.	1	2	3	4	5
41. Customer service is provided that is second to none.	1	2	3	4	5
42. There is a fair system for evaluating individual performance.	1	2	3	4	5
43. It is always clear why someone deserves promotion.	1	2	3	4	5
44. I trust my staff to use their own judgement.	1	2	3	4	5
45. My staff all understand how their plans link to the section's objectives.	1	2	3	4	5
46. I understand how my role contributes to the organisation's success.	1	2	3	4	5
47. Everyone is informed about what is going on.	1	2	3	4	5
48. I can take appropriate decisions within the context of my job without seeking approval.	1	2	3	4	5
49. As a manager, I regularly use appraisal information to help improve my staff's performance.	1	2	3	4	5
50. Changes in the organisation's annual plan seem to have no affect on me.	1	2	3	4	5
51. My staff are clear about my role.	1	2	3	4	5
52. Poor performance should be reflected in pay.	1	2	3	4	5
53. Initiative is taken to get things done.	1	2	3	4	5
54. Integrity is a real part of the organisation's management style.	1	2	3	4	5
55. I have had my work strongly criticised in the past.	1	2	3	4	5
56. My annual appraisal is more a reflection of my recent rather than annual performance.	1	2	3	4	5
57. Everyone is treated with trust and respect.	1	2	3	4	5
58. Promotion is a good measure of past performance.	1	2	3	4	5
59. I know what I must do to ensure the organisation achieves its aims.	1	2	3	4	5
60. Decision making is made at appropriate levels.	1	2	3	4	5

My current view is

	strongly disagree		neutral		strongly agree
61. The pay structure should include an element to reward length of service.	1	2	3	4	5
62. I am clear what the organisation's plans are.	1	2	3	4	5
63. I am clear about what the organisation's pay policy is.	1	2	3	4	5
64. Training clearly links to performance improvement.	1	2	3	4	5
65. Rewarding careers are on offer.	1	2	3	4	5
66. There is pressure to hit targets.	1	2	3	4	5
67. I believe my appraisal is a fair assessment of how well I have been performing.	1	2	3	4	5
68. As a manager, I really tackle poor performance.	1	2	3	4	5
69. I am confident that my performance will be adequately rewarded by my manager.	1	2	3	4	5
70. Customer needs are approached creatively.	1	2	3	4	5
71. I know what the organisation's goals are.	1	2	3	4	5
72. My manager frequently checks my work.	1	2	3	4	5
73. The planning process provides business focus.	1	2	3	4	5
74. Timely and effective feedback is given and received.	1	2	3	4	5
75. Pay within this company helps retain people.	1	2	3	4	5
76. I receive enough support from my manager to carry out my job.	1	2	3	4	5
77. If I had performed poorly, I would not expect a pay increase.	1	2	3	4	5
78. People are developed to their full potential.	1	2	3	4	5
79. The current appraisal system clearly differentiates on performance.	1	2	3	4	5
80. I am confident that high performance will result in promotion.	1	2	3	4	5
81. I know what the organisation considers to be priority areas for personal improvement.	1	2	3	4	5
82. Staff are inspired to develop and achieve goals.	1	2	3	4	5
83. I feel free to exercise my own judgement.	1	2	3	4	5

My current view is

	strongly disagree		neutral		strongly agree
84. I am clear how the organisation's objectives are linked to mine.	1	2	3	4	5
85. Pay within this company helps attract people.	1	2	3	4	5
86. The highest professional standards are adopted.	1	2	3	4	5
87. It is mentioned when I have done a good job.	1	2	3	4	5
88. As a manager, I am able to use the current pay system to motivate my staff.	1	2	3	4	5
89. The 'best' performers are clearly identifiable.	1	2	3	4	5
90. Managers have used the annual appraisal system to criticise my performance.	1	2	3	4	5
91. People are listened to with an open mind.	1	2	3	4	5
92. I am confident that I will be given recognition by my manager for good performance.	1	2	3	4	5
93. I understand how my actions impact on my section's performance.	1	2	3	4	5
94. I have sufficient freedom to adjust my behaviour to improve performance.	1	2	3	4	5
95. My subordinates and I agree on what their job responsibilities are.	1	2	3	4	5
96. I know how I can help the organisation achieve its goals.	1	2	3	4	5
97. Pay reflects length of service more than performance.	1	2	3	4	5
98. It is mentioned when I have done a bad job.	1	2	3	4	5
99. I let my staff know at the right time their work is unacceptable.	1	2	3	4	5
100. Working together is encouraged to ensure everyone wins.	1	2	3	4	5
101. Unnecessary demands are placed on staff.	1	2	3	4	5
102. The appraisal process helps me to improve my performance.	1	2	3	4	5
103. Promotion is primarily a factor of good performance.	1	2	3	4	5

My current view is

	strongly disagree		neutral		strongly agree
104. I know how my behaviour affects my department's performance.	1	2	3	4	5
105. I am free to adjust the use of my resources as I see fit.	1	2	3	4	5
106. I am clear how my budget links to the organisation's.	1	2	3	4	5
107. My manager adequately explains how my pay is calculated.	1	2	3	4	5
108. Information is shared at all levels.	1	2	3	4	5
109. I have no doubt as to how the standards of my work will be judged.	1	2	3	4	5
110. The elements of the appraisal process are clearly linked to business objectives.	1	2	3	4	5
111. The appraisal system assures me that my performance will be recognised.	1	2	3	4	5
112. I know how my actions impact on my operating company's performance.	1	2	3	4	5
113. I feel free to take independent actions necessary to carry out my job.	1	2	3	4	5
114. I am clear about my manager's plans.	1	2	3	4	5
115. I feel my pay is a good reflection of my performance.	1	2	3	4	5
116. My manager fully explains why decisions have been made.	1	2	3	4	5
117. I have been strongly reprimanded for delivering below standard in the past.	1	2	3	4	5
118. I would be happy for judgements to be passed on my performance on the basis of the appraisal system.	1	2	3	4	5
119. The appraisal system assures me that good performance will lead to promotion.	1	2	3	4	5
120. I understand how my behaviour affects the organisation's performance.	1	2	3	4	5
121. My manager trusts me to use my own judgement.	1	2	3	4	5
122. I understand how my plans link to my section's objectives.	1	2	3	4	5
123. My subordinates are confident that I will adequately reward their performance.	1	2	3	4	5

My current view is

	strongly disagree		neutral		strongly agree
124. The pay system is flexible enough to reward truly outstanding performance.	1	2	3	4	5
125. I have ample opportunity to influence decisions which affect the way I do my job.	1	2	3	4	5
126. I frequently check my staff's work.	1	2	3	4	5
127. I know how quality is measured in this organisation.	1	2	3	4	5
128. Managers regularly use appraisal information to help improve performance.	1	2	3	4	5
129. The appraisal system assures me that my performance will be rewarded.	1	2	3	4	5
130. I provide my staff with sufficient support to ensure they can successfully carry out their jobs.	1	2	3	4	5
131. I am clear about the role of my manager.	1	2	3	4	5
132. The structure encourages the use of initiative.	1	2	3	4	5
133. There is clear link between my plans and how I will be rewarded.	1	2	3	4	5

APPENDIX 2b

DIAGNOSING YOUR CURRENT PERFORMANCE MANAGEMENT PROCESS

WHERE ARE YOU NOW?

To understand what the next moves need to be in improving performance management, organisations need to ask questions such as:

- ❑ How sure are we about what excellent performance really looks like?
- ❑ How do we currently manage and reward performance?
  - annual individual performance appraisal?
  - personal development planning?
  - a range of reward/recognition elements?
  - an integrated performance management process?
- ❑ When did we last review our approach?
- ❑ What did our last attitude survey tell us about this area?

IF YOU HAVE AN APPRAISAL SCHEME

- ❑ Who owns the scheme:
  - the personnel/HR function?
  - line managers/employees?

- ❑ If you ask people how it works do they:
  - produce the forms and tell you how they get filled in?
  - tell you what the key processes are?
  - tell you what they have got out of it in terms of personal/team performance improvement?
- ❑ Which elements of performance are covered:
  - objectives linked to the strategic plan cascaded through the organisation?
  - skills/competencies required to work effectively?
  - competencies specifically linked to high performance?
- ❑ Is the scheme decaying in terms of:
  - it is a ritual that has become an annual burden?
  - the forms only get filled in because managers' performance rewards depend on getting paperwork done?
  - the debate on performance within the organisation happens elsewhere?
- ❑ Is what we do viewed with:
  - enthusiasm?
  - commitment?
  - cynicism?
  - apprehension?
- ❑ Do we have the same process and underlying values for employees at all levels?
- ❑ Does this work, or are needs different?
- ❑ Do people feel comfortable with our approach to performance rating?
- ❑ Do managers use ratings as rewards? Is there 'rating drift'?
- ❑ Do people feel that they put in a lot of effort just to produce a rating for the merit pay scheme?
- ❑ How do people readjust objective and refocus performance as needed through the year?
- ❑ How good are the links with developing and training?

OVERALL PERFORMANCE MANAGEMENT

- ❑ How do our top executives manage performance? Is this consistent with our overall approach?
- ❑ What approach do we use for managing team performance? Does it really get to the heart of understanding interdependencies between team members?
- ❑ What are we doing about professionals/specialists or areas where we have very large spans of control?
- ❑ Do we have processes for:
  - planning performance improvement and development which are integrated into the way the organisation is managed?
  - managing and coaching performance through the year?
  - reviewing/appraising performance which pulls together people's work on their own and their work with others?
  - ensuring that each individual looks to the future performance and not just the previous year?
  - recognising and rewarding performance using the full range of rewards available within the organisation?
- ❑ Do we take account of our customers', or rather, stockholders' views of our performance, both internal and external to the organisation?
- ❑ How effective are the links with our total quality/customer service initiatives?
- ❑ How do we benchmark our standards against best practice, both internally and externally in the interests of continuous learning and performance improvement?
- ❑ What are we doing about working on the climate and management styles needed within the organisation to enable performance improvement?
- ❑ How well are we communicating what we do and keeping it alive?

Finding answers to these is the way organisations build understanding of where they have got to and what needs to be explored and achieved for the future. Then they can commit themselves to transforming what they do.

Index